Finding Emelyn

Finding Emelyn

How I Connected with a Past Life, the Other Side, and My Purpose

Diane Richards

Printed in the United States of America

First Printing, 2021

ISBN–13: 978–1–949001–22–8 print edition
ISBN–13: 978–1–949001–23–5 ebook edition

Waterside Productions
2055 Oxford Ave
Cardiff, CA 92007
www.waterside.com

This book is dedicated to my incredibly supportive husband, Jay Mark and my three beautiful children, Michale Jay, Jennifer Milagros, and Michael John. A very special thank you to Emelyn, who guided me through to a new chapter of life.

Praise for *Finding Emelyn*

What an amazing and unexpected joy it was to read *Finding Emelyn: How I Connected with a Past Life, the Other Side, and my Purpose.* What Diane Richards has given us is nothing short of a jaw-dropping experience into the heart of her life—who she is … and was … at Soul level! As she lays out the experiences of her life and the traumas she endured, you can't help but feel the anguish she had no choice but to accept. Her vulnerability as she lays bare her struggles is so refreshing and so real—you marvel at the courage it took for her to tell her story of love and loss, struggle and pain…and then, finally, as she envelops you in her transformative discoveries, you rejoice with her! I cried with her, I laughed with her, I rejoiced with her, and I feared for her. I cried again, then I laughed again, and then my mouth gaped open and eyes flew wide as I found myself asking, "How on earth could this be true?" Then she showed me that this journey was, indeed … undeniably TRUE! Diane takes you on the spiritual ride of your life as she carries you with her, visually, inside the synchronicities and unexpected discoveries that had been waiting for her before "she was born as Diane." *Finding Emelyn* was the impetus for Diane finding the "Diane of her dreams"—the woman she always knew she was but could never touch! I found this book to be inspirational, transformational, and extremely thought provoking—all in equal amounts. Well worth the read. Matter of fact, I read it twice to make sure I hadn't missed even one moment of this intriguing, life-altering book. I highly recommend it for anyone searching for their own answers to the "Whys" of their own lives.

—Dr. Sharon Prentice, best-selling author of *Becoming Starlight: Surviving Grief and Mending the Wounds of Loss*

"I couldn't put this book down! It is an amazing and descriptive accounting of a journey into a past life memory that the author was able to historically trace across the country and propel her through over ten decades of time. This process opened up a spiritual journey that evolved into forgiveness, self healing, and the gift and ability to read and heal others."

—Pat Longo, international spiritual healer and author of *The Gifts Beneath Your Anxiety: Simple Spiritual Tools to Find Peace, Awaken the Power Within, and Heal Your Life*

"*Finding Emelyn: How I Connected with a Past Life, the Other Side, and my Purpose is a* compelling memoir by Diane Richards, one of the country's most gifted mediums. The book is a fascinating journey into her spiritual development that involves unraveling layers of past and present in ways that heal the heart and open the doors to life's greatest mysteries. Diane shares her story honestly and credibly inspiring the hope that all of us can experience greater insight into our childhoods, lives we lived before, and the source of all creation where Spirit resides. If you are seeking a deeply inspiring read, reach for *Finding Emelyn.*

—*Lisa Smartt, M.A.,* author of *Words at the Threshold* and *Cante Bardo*

Table of Contents

Acknowledgements

This book would not have been possible without the many people who have helped and supported me, not only in this writing journey but in life.

Thank you to Carol Hammer and Lisa Fugard for your expertise editing skills and seeing my vision.

Thank you to Waterside Productions, Inc, and their amazing staff. I really appreciate the opportunity you have given me. A special shout out to Josh Freel for answering all my publishing questions and accommodating all my changes.

Jacob Cooper, MSW, I am eternally grateful for your support and giving me your infamous pep talks (or kick in the ass!) when needed. Thank you for all you did to make this publication possible.

James Caskey, author and owner of Savannah, Georgia's Cobblestone Tours, thank you for taking the time to meet with me and review my story during the early phases of development. Also, Murray Silver, author of Great Balls of Fire: *The Uncensored Story of Jerry Lee Lewis,* for showing me the flavor of Savannah and teaching me how to tell a story.

I am extremely grateful to Dr. Sharon Prentice, Suzanne Giesemann, Pat Longo, and Lisa Smartt for taking the time to read my story and write such heart-felt reviews. To have endorsements from such dedicated, strong, respected and talented women is extremely humbling. Thank you!

Thank you to the amazing staff at Savannah, Georgia's Historical Society who helped me find the treasures that brought me to Emelyn. Your professional guidance taught me a great deal about research. The time spent in the breathtaking Historical Society building was a gift that I am forever grateful to have experienced. Thank you to Alex Raskin Antiques, Savannah, Georgia for allowing me the opportunity to explore the house of my past life regression.

Thank you to my many friends and clients who have supported me along this path. I thank you for trusting and allowing me to connect with your loved ones. It is an honor. Thank you Bobby Marshuetz for reuniting me with your sister, Patricia and being a huge catalyst in my life changing journey.

It is with much appreciation and admiration that I thank my teachers and mentors; Dr. Brian Weiss, Tony Stockwell, Janet Nohavec, Colin Bates, Dr. Carol Carbone, Joe Shiel, James Van Praagh and the tutors from Arthur Findlay College. You continue to inspire me to be my best, stay grounded and work for the greater good.

No-one has been more important to me in the pursuit of this project than the members of my family. I can't thank my husband, Jay Mark, enough for his faith which supported me throughout this venture. You encourage me to be me, providing opportunities for my continued growth. I would like to give a special thank you to my mother, whose love and guidance are with me in whatever I pursue. Throughout all of life's ups and downs, my mother continues to be there. That says it all. I love you.

And to Spirit, without whom this book could not have been written. Thank you for trusting me with your stories, your secrets, your guidance and your wisdom. Thank you for helping me remove my blinders and guiding me to a life built on faith and love.

PROLOGUE

My story keeps surprising me.

I emerged from a childhood filled with family turmoil and discouraging teachers to become a successful educator and founder of an alternative school in New Jersey. If that were not enough, I surprised myself by discovering what I can only describe as convincing evidence that I lived another life in the 19th century that eerily paralleled mine, even though it unfolded in a Southern culture foreign to my Northeastern roots. That was followed by startling indications that I have a talent for communicating messages from people who have died, which rang true to me as I looked back on childhood experiences that I had suppressed in the face of adult judgment.

But the biggest and most meaningful surprise, the one that I believe will resonate even with skeptics of the mystical, was how hard – and yet how easy — it was to find my purpose in life. I had worked so obsessively on my career and had identified with a materialistic world of "should" and "must" for so long that opening my heart scared me. Yet once I began identifying with the soul, I began to heal – and to help others with their healing.

I am not here to convince anyone to believe in past lives, mediums, meditation, or ancient healing practices. I am here to share my journey and, perhaps, to open minds to a new way of seeing. There are many paths to awakening your soul and discovering your True Self. This was mine.

Note To Readers: This story reflects my recollection of events. In a few cases I have noted that I did not use a person's real name so as to protect that person's privacy. Dialogue has been recreated from memory.

Part I: Past Lives

We are products of our past, but we don't have to be prisoners of it.
— *Rick Warren, The Purpose Driven Life: What on Earth Am I Here for?*

Chapter 1: Confronting Myself

Our hearts know the path to happiness and inner peace. Spiritual practices such as meditation and prayer are designed to remind us of what we already know. — *Dr. Brian Weiss*

It was after eight o'clock in the evening when I pulled the van into the driveway of our home in suburban New Jersey, opened the garage door, and stepped into the kitchen. My husband Mark was standing there, alone, shaking his head.

"You forgot, didn't you?" he said. "You forgot. How could you?"

"What's the matter? What did I forget?" I demanded. "Where's Jennifer?"

"She's upstairs in her room, getting ready for bed," he said quietly. "Tonight was her concert at school. I held dinner. We waited for you as long we could. You promised you would come straight home tonight."

I felt as if I had been hit in the chest with a sledgehammer. I had completely forgotten. The only thing I had on my mind was work. I had forgotten my six-year-old daughter's concert at school – a concert she had been rehearsing and couldn't wait to share. A concert I had promised I would not miss. Mark had even reminded me earlier that afternoon before a school field trip that took me out of cell phone range. I was so upset I couldn't move.

"Don't worry. I covered for you," I heard Mark saying. His voice sounded miles away although he was standing only a few feet from me. "I told her you called and were going to meet us at her school.

I told her I was going to save you a seat. I could tell the whole time she was on stage that she was preoccupied with looking for you. She just wanted to see your face. Then the concert ended and I met her backstage, but you still weren't there. Don't worry. I covered that, too. I told her you got to the concert late, but that you were there, in the back of the auditorium, standing. I told her that you love her, that you are proud of her and would see her at home."

I looked up at my husband. "How could I have forgotten? How did I let this happen?"

Mark picked up a folded piece of paper from the counter and handed it to me. It was the concert program.

"Here," he said. "I got this for you so you would at least know the songs she performed with her class. If she knew you weren't there, it would break her heart."

What was I doing? I had just spent this mid-December evening of 2009 with other school staff members, giving my best to other people's children while I neglected my own. There was no excuse. I was in the habit of working late each night. With after-school enrichment programs and the never-ending mounds of paper work, I would immerse myself in the tasks at hand, not paying attention to the time, sometimes working until after midnight.

This night, the after-school agenda had consisted of a history exploration activity, followed by pizza at a local restaurant. As I had headed the school van in the direction of my house, I had glanced at the clock and noticed with satisfaction that it was seven p.m. I would be home before eight-thirty. An early night. The students had been returned snug and safe to their homes, leaving the van empty and quiet. I turned up the heat, put on my favorite CD and listened to Stevie Nicks' haunting voice wooing me with the magical words of Rhiannon as I began my long journey home. The moon was difficult to see in the partly cloudy sky, but its glow peeked through, showing its reflection against the slushy snow that lay on the ground, providing a warm light to the cool evening.

My school was my life. I couldn't remember a time without my dream of opening a school, but I had deliberately waited until my son was in middle school before I took on the daunting challenge. Jennifer was not yet in our lives. I had put all my time and energy into birthing the school. I had lost sight of my priorities.

Pushing myself into a never-ending frenzy seemed normal to me. I had grown up seeing it as my only way out of a life I disliked. I began babysitting, delivering newspapers, house sitting, plant sitting, and pet sitting as a young girl. In high school, I worked as many hours as possible at a fast food restaurant and a supermarket. During college, I worked at the supermarket from four p.m. until after midnight, only to get up each morning to attend classes from eight a.m. until three p.m. After college, I worked full time as a teacher, continued working part-time at the supermarket and pursued part-time graduate studies.

Never had I entertained the thought that maybe what I was doing wasn't healthy. As I stood in my kitchen that night, holding the program from my daughter's concert, something jarred loose inside me. I allowed myself to consider that perhaps this lifestyle I had developed was not working.

"Mommy!" I heard Jennifer shout as she ran down the stairs and into the kitchen. I scooped her up in my arms and held her tightly. "What was your favorite song, Mommy?" she asked excitedly as I let her go from my embrace and gently placed her on the floor. Before I could answer, Jennifer was on to her next question. "Could you see me on stage, Mommy? Could you? I was looking for you in the audience, but I didn't see you. I'm sorry you had to stand in the back! I was so worried you weren't going to be able to come to the show. I was afraid you would have a meeting."

She took a breath, gave me a quick hug, and skipped out of the room. "Come on, Mom! Let's read a story before I go to bed! I'm glad you're home."

Feeling like a dog who knows he's in trouble, I followed my daughter up the stairs. We chose two books and took turns reading to one another. As we turned the last page, I tucked Jennifer into bed. As I leaned over to kiss her goodnight, her big brown eyes met mine.

"You are the best Mommy in the whole world!" Jennifer said, as the love on her face washed over me.

"You are the best daughter in the world," I replied. "I am so lucky to have you in my life!"

"Thank you, Mommy!" she said as she closed her eyes, falling asleep with a smile on her face.

I felt like a fraud, undeserving of her accolades and overwhelmed with guilt at my dishonesty and neglect. I walked, sulking, into my bedroom, and Mark embraced me.

"I am a horrible mother," I said.

"No, you're not," he said, giving me kindness I didn't want to accept. "You work hard to provide for your family. It wasn't as though you were just out and about. You were working."

I pulled away, not convinced. "This has got to stop," I said, sighing. "I thought having the school would make me happy, yet I'm not happy. It's taken over my life. I feel like I should be single, with no other responsibilities, to be able to run the school. Instead of feeling blessed by what I have, I feel burdened and resentful."

"You're just feeling this way because you missed her concert," Mark said. "There will be other concerts. Don't be so hard on yourself. Get ready for bed, and I'll go make you a cup of tea."

I stood in the quiet of my bedroom, listening to Mark's footsteps as he descended the stairs to the kitchen. I knew I was feeling more than momentary guilt. This feeling had churned in my stomach many times throughout the years, but I had never acknowledged what it was. As I stood alone, I heard a voice within clearly say, "Follow your heart."

That December night, for the first time in a long time, I knelt next to my bed, closed my eyes, and prayed. I asked God to guide me, to help me, to forgive me for losing focus on what was most important.

In the next months, the nagging voice grew louder. I had invested all I had financially, physically, and emotionally into creating the school. I believed in its mission. The workload, politics, and responsibilities were killing me, but I feared failure, feared looking crazy for throwing away all these years of energy and money. The extra pounds, the headaches, the fatigue, the back pain, the illnesses, the high blood pressure, the stress in my family relationships all screamed at me to stop doing this. Politics, policies, and outside forces scraped away at my confidence.

But my ears might as well have been stuffed with cotton. My emotions and intuition were buried under rationalizations: "Don't be irresponsible." "Your husband is working full-time now at the school, so your family can't afford for you to quit." "People are counting on you." "Everyone will think you're crazy."

The nagging voice inside me did not give up. The more I suppressed it, the stronger it got, until one day, it wormed its way inside and got the upper hand. I decided to attend a workshop that would change my life.

Chapter 2: Saying Yes

That which is impenetrable to us really exists. Behind the secrets of nature remains something subtle, intangible, and inexplicable. Veneration for this force beyond anything that we can comprehend is my religion. — Albert Einstein (1879 – 1955)

"What are you doing this weekend?" Tracey, my friend and neighbor, asked when I answered the phone. It was February 2010, and the ground was covered with large mounds of snow. The winter had been long, cold, and depressing, and I was hoping this most recent snowstorm would be the last of the season.

"Nothing much," I said. "Probably just working, as usual."

"Remember that book I told you about, Many Lives, Many Masters by Dr. Brian Weiss?" my friend said.

She had spoken of it often. Dr. Weiss had been a traditional psychologist until he experienced a patient recalling past lives while under hypnosis. Since then, Dr. Weiss had written several books on past lives. His view is that resolving issues in a past life can help a person's present life become healthier and more fulfilling.

"Yes, I remember. Why do you ask?"

"Well, Dr. Weiss will be in Philadelphia this weekend presenting a workshop," Tracey said. "I found out there are still tickets available and thought we could go. What do you think?"

For some reason, I didn't hesitate. "Yes! Let's do it. Let's go."

"Great!" Tracey said. "The workshop begins early Saturday morning, so I thought we could leave late Friday afternoon and stay in a hotel near the convention center. Would that work for you?"

Once again, without hesitation, I answered, "Yes! And if not, I'll make it work. Book the tickets and the hotel, and I'll pick you up around 3:30 tomorrow afternoon."

It was out of the norm for me to accept an invitation to do something for me, for fun. I had committed to going away for the weekend without even consulting my husband. I had committed to leaving work early on Friday. Why had I agreed so easily without my usual inner monologue about all the reasons I shouldn't go, about why work should come before play? Why didn't I feel the usual guilt at taking time just for myself? I chalked it up to really needing a break and put it behind me.

My husband has always been very supportive of my endeavors, so his "Go. Have a fun time. I'll take care of things at home" response was no surprise. Mark's strength has been in taking care of our children. He has always cooked, done laundry, shopped and handled various other household chores that I found mundane. When our son was a baby, Mark never thought twice about changing a diaper. Maybe this is more common now, but many of my envious friends claimed their husbands would never touch a dirty diaper and had no idea how to change one. Mark's support and domestic abilities allowed me to go to graduate school, work full time, pursue continuing education in addiction counseling, open a school, and provide consistent financial support for our family. He allowed me to fulfill my need to be someone.

Although I had wanted to teach ever since I was a child creating a classroom in my family's basement, I purposely waited for what I thought was the perfect timing to open my own school. Once my son reached middle school, he was old enough to need less of my time. My husband had been working at the same job with a good company for several years, so his stable position with a decent salary allowed me to stop teaching full time and gave me the flexibility to develop my school. So I left full-time employment, took on some consulting and tutoring work, and began creating my dream school. But within a few weeks of leaving my job and committing to the overwhelming task of opening a state-approved school, Mark lost his job. I had learned that there is no such thing as planning the perfect time.

After my phone call with Tracey, I went to the bookshelf in our home office and looked for the paperback by Dr. Weiss. I hadn't read the book but knew I had picked up a copy quite some time ago, after Tracey spoke so highly of it. I sat in the armchair, curled up my legs, and opened the book. Once I began, I didn't stop.

As a child, I never questioned past lives. I just knew it as fact and assumed everyone else did, too. I had memories, thoughts, and feelings that I never doubted were connected to my previous lives. I played dress-up in period costumes and recreated the scenes in my head. As an adult, I had lost touch with these memories.

When I was young, I loved going to the gift shop where my mother worked. The shop had beautiful items such as fine crystal and delicate china patterns that most children would not find fascinating, but I loved to look at them. I was always drawn to the patterns with delicate flowers of blue around the edging. I loved to imagine a long dining table, elegantly set with blue-flowered fine china and etched crystal glassware. As I stared longingly at the china, the same scene would play over and over again in my head.

I would see myself in a beautiful Southern mansion in the 1800s, wearing a deep blue dress with a white petticoat and bloomers. My blonde hair was in ringlets with blue ribbons pulling back the sides. I would be standing in the hallway of this beautiful home, peering into the large dining room. The room was massive with stunning floor-to-ceiling windows. Candelabras adorned with crystal pendants flanked the marble fireplace. I was fascinated by the rainbows that reflected on the cream-colored walls when the sun hit the crystal pendants.

I was careful to be extremely quiet and blend into the wall of the hallway as best I could. Children were not privy to the adult dining experience. This social gathering of the Southern elite was no place for children. I watched, mesmerized, as the servants brought out sweet-smelling platters of food. The women at the table were so elaborately dressed and the men so distinguished. The table was elegantly set with blue-flowered china and silverware for every course. I watched as the guests raised their etched crystal glasses, giving toasts to prosperity and wellness.

"Child! What are you doing peeking in on the grown folks?" It was my Mammy. "You know you are not to disturb their party. Now go on upstairs so we can get you ready for bed. Praise the Lord, child, someday the wrong person is going to find you sneaking around this house, spying on things that are none of your business."

I couldn't help it. I was mesmerized by things that I was unable to be part of or embrace. I would creep around that mansion, watching, learning, and imprinting what I saw.

This trait from a life of long ago had stayed with me in this life. As a child, I had carefully followed my father around the house, fascinated by someone I was not privy to, a man I could not embrace.

I finished reading most of the book, Many Lives, Many Masters, skimming through some of the chapters. I put it back on the bookcase and went downstairs to make myself my nightly cup of tea. I poured the boiling water over the teabag and into the mug, adding just the right amount of sugar and milk. I brought the mug upstairs, set it on the table next to my bed and slipped into my pajamas. My husband was already in bed, sitting with remote in hand, flipping through the channels, in search of the perfect, mindless television show to put him to sleep.

As I crawled under the covers and arranged my pillows to support me while I sat in bed, I asked Mark, "Do you believe in past lives? Do you think we continue in some way after we physically leave this earth?"

Without taking his eyes off the television, he said, "Yeah, I guess so. It makes sense. It would explain why someone might be considered more of an old soul while another is still a newbie. Perhaps the old souls have been recycled several times. I don't really know too much about past lives, ghosts, or the spirit world, but after hearing some of your experiences, I definitely believe there is a lot more going on out there that most people don't see."

His answer took me by surprise. "What experiences are you talking about?" I said.

He was still looking at the television and seemed exasperated that I was disturbing him from finding his mindless show. "Do we have to talk about this now? It's after midnight, and we have to get up early for work tomorrow. We need to get some sleep."

"Just give me one example, and I'll leave you alone," I pleaded.

"Well, how do you explain what happened when your grandmother died? Or what about your father's death? There has to be some type of energy that continues in order for things like that to occur. Although, you might just be some sort of freak, because these experiences don't happen to me! But since I know that what you've experienced is true, I am a believer. Now get to sleep."

My husband put down the remote, leaving the Comedy Channel blaring, and within minutes he was snoring. I sat in bed, sipping my tea and replaying my father's and my grandmother's deaths in my mind. But as usual, the demands of life prevented me from entertaining these thoughts and memories for very long. Tomorrow was a busy day, and I needed sleep so I could function. Over the years, I had become well versed at pushing my thoughts aside. I took my last sip of tea, turned out the lights, and welcomed the darkness of sleep.

Chapter 3: Turning Point

We are not our bodies. We have existed before we came into our physical bodies and will exist after we leave these bodies. And we will go on. — *Dr. Brian Weiss*

The morning of our trip to Philadelphia, I woke up early and packed an overnight bag. Was I really going through with this? After reading Dr. Weiss' book the night before, I was interested in hearing him speak and learning more about his thoughts and philosophy.

Tearing myself away from work was extremely difficult for me, yet as soon as all the students had left the school and the last bus had safely pulled away at the end of the day, I exited the building and left work behind. I pulled into Tracey's driveway a little before 3:30 p.m., eager to get on the road and begin our journey.

Tracey and I were at no loss for conversation during our long ride to Philadelphia. As we chatted, I was completely caught off guard when Tracey asked, "You realize that Dr. Weiss is going to put us under and help us recall past life experiences, don't you?"

No, I had not realized this. I thought I was going to a lecture. I thought he would talk about his latest book and experiences. I didn't comprehend that I was attending an experiential workshop!

"Oh, no," I said. "I'm sure he'll only select one or two audience members to volunteer as a demonstration, but he won't attempt to put the whole audience under. Will he?"

"Yes," Tracey said. "I believe he uses his techniques on the whole audience."

I had a hard time grasping that. How would that work? Would that work? I remembered as a little girl telling my mom I wanted to remember all my lives and asking her if I could be hypnotized. Of course she didn't support this type of thinking, and I didn't pursue it. Now, here I was, an adult, and I might be presented with the opportunity to recall past lives. Why was I apprehensive? Why was I in doubt of something I had felt so strongly about as a child?

After we arrived in Philadelphia and checked into our hotel, Tracey and I headed to dinner. The recent snowstorm had left the restaurant in a bad place, with menu items missing because food couldn't be delivered. Some servers hadn't shown up for work. But despite the limited choices and slow service, we settled into a relaxing and enjoyable evening. It had been too long since I experienced a dinner out that wasn't work-related.

After dinner we returned to our rooms. We had to be at the convention center early in the morning. We would meet at the hotel's restaurant for breakfast before the workshop. As I lay in bed, awaiting sleep to overcome my body, I couldn't help but be a little anxious about what might transpire during the workshop.

In the morning, the hotel restaurant was bustling with people looking for a morning fix of caffeine or a quick bite to start their day. Tracey and I snagged a table, and I immediately ordered coffee, which was usually all I had in the morning. Tracey, a disciplined eater, drank her decaffeinated beverage with her healthy whole grains and fruit, while I dumped my sixth package of sugar and second container of cream into my coffee. The restaurant was humming with activity, which made it difficult for us to hold a conversation. We finished our breakfast and headed directly across the street to the convention center.

After checking in, we walked into Dr. Weiss' workshop. The room was already filled with hundreds of people. Tracey and I found two seats near the center of the room. It wasn't long before Dr. Weiss took the stage. He spent a short time introducing himself and filling the audience in on his background and experiences. Within no time, he asked the audience to please get comfortable and invited us to find a spot on the floor. He encouraged us all to relax and even lie down if we chose. Tracey was right. Dr. Weiss was going to use his past life regression techniques on everyone. I was still skeptical about how this would work. I thought this was something that had to take place one-on-one in the privacy of a doctor's or counselor's office.

Tracey and I left our chairs and found a spot where we could sit on the floor and lean against the back wall. As soon as everyone was settled, the lights dimmed and the sound of relaxing music filled the room. Dr. Weiss began to speak in a soothing voice, giving our minds directions to follow. Before long, my eyes were closed, and I felt myself drifting to another realm. I soon saw swirls of color in my mind as I focused on Dr. Weiss' voice. All other noises and distractions were inaudible to me. Dr. Weiss relaxed us with guided imagery, walking us down a large staircase and into a beautiful garden. His voice helped relax every muscle and calmed my busy mind until I lay in a semi-comatose state, relaxed but with focused concentration.

"While your body rests in the garden, let us go back in time," instructed Dr. Weiss. "There is no limit to your memory. You can go back as far as you wish. There is no limit. You can remember everything."

Images began to come to me, and I was soon carried away to another time and place. The memory was so real, so vivid, that not only did I see it play out before me, I felt it throughout my body.

I was in a carriage, a landau, sitting across from another young girl who I felt was a relative, perhaps a sister or a cousin. We were both wearing our finest dresses, and the many layers of clothes were making my nine-year-old body itch. I was eager to escape the carriage and stretch my legs. The church service had been lengthy, and I had been sitting for far too long. The young girl with me sensed my restlessness and gave me a look of exasperation. The carriage stopped in front of a grand home. As the driver took my hand to help me down, I noticed a puddle in the street, left from the rain the day before. My father must have read my mind and gave me a stern look that immediately told me I was to walk around the puddle and not jump in it, as I so desired.

My father was a stately man, elegantly dressed in his dark tailcoat, vest, and white shirt with winged collar. His dark mustache was neatly groomed, and his dark sideburns seemed to be escaping from underneath his black top hat. His stance was impressive as he stood tall, with his walking stick in one hand, observing me as I descended from the carriage and obediently restrained myself from stepping in the puddle or dirtying my Sunday clothes.

I admired my father. He was a well-respected businessman in high social standing. My father was a leader, a protector, and a provider. He was involved in many business dealings and provided a high-class lifestyle for his family – a lifestyle that allowed us to have many servants, that allowed my mother to stay in bed for most of the day, absent from her children.

I heard Dr. Weiss's soothing voice directing me away from this memory and moving me forward in time. "If you wish to go further, we can do that now," he gently suggested. "Go to significant events. Spend as much time as you need and find the answers." I took a few deep breaths and soon found myself lost in another memory of this same lifetime.

There was not much of a breeze on the beach this afternoon. I slowly followed behind my father and the woman with him, not taking my eyes off the woman with one hand holding her parasol and the other clinging to my father's arm. I did allow my eyes to wander occasionally towards the tall, white lighthouse, which represented to me guidance and strength, both of which I valued in my life. During the months since my mother had died, I had taken on more responsibility in overseeing my siblings. I was barely fourteen years old, but I took the role of being the eldest daughter very seriously. I looked on as my father's companion chose a spot and laid the blanket on the beach. I released my sisters' hands from mine and watched them run towards the blanket. This new woman in my father's life was no more than four years older than me and younger than my oldest brother. I looked at her as someone not ready to be a wife and mother. I was not ready to accept her with my father. I was engulfed in feelings of sadness, loneliness, and responsibility. I took off my shoes and headed toward the ocean, eager to feel the wet sand and water between my toes. I stood at the edge of the ocean, and a slight breeze blew the skirt of my navy blue bathing suit as the waves gently splashed over my feet. I looked out into the depth of the ocean and realized that this new woman would soon be my father's wife. It would be a lie to say that what I was feeling was happiness.

"If you wish, you can move forward in time and find out what happens to you," Dr. Weiss said. "Are there any traumas? Is there a death scene? If you wish not to view this, then do not. Just float above. You can see more than one lifetime if you choose, or you can stay and examine one in more detail."

I chose to stay and examine in more detail. I moved forward once again and found myself at the end of my life. I was in an apartment in a city. It felt like New York. I saw myself in my bedroom, lying in bed, looking out the window and reflecting on my life.

I could hear my dear friend in the kitchen making tea and talking to my nephew and his wife in hushed tones. I sighed deeply, feeling thankful they were with me. I had never married. I had no children. I had moved away from my family. My work was my life, and the people I worked with became my family. Since retiring, I had felt lost. Since the passing of my closest friend and companion, I had felt alone. Lost and alone. I had done some traveling, reconnected with family, and enjoyed it, but working was my passion. Without it, I couldn't help but feel empty. Teaching and running a school had allowed me to surround myself with children who filled the void of having no children of my own, and the staff had filled my need for family. The person who had worked by my side and shared all this with me was gone, adding to my sadness.

I closed my eyes and enjoyed the warm September breeze as it wafted in through my slightly opened window and glided across my face. I could smell the ending of summer and the beginning of a new school year. I missed preparing for the academic year. Even more, I missed by dearest friend and colleague who had worked with me and retired with me. She was gone. I was ready to go, too.

I was startled as my nephew and his wife entered my room carrying a tray with a pot of tea and a small plate of cookies. I took a long look at my nephew and smiled. He was a handsome man with a kind heart. He sat on the edge of my bed and took my hand. For a moment, our eyes met, and we both knew. I gently squeezed his hand, hoping to reassure him I was at peace. I turned my head to face the window. I could hear the sounds of children playing, dogs barking, cars honking, and people talking. I could feel the city within my reach. I could hear the sounds of life. I was suddenly overwhelmed with fatigue. It was time to close my eyes. It was time to end this chapter. It was time to move on.

"Imagine that you are now finishing up and leaving this time and returning to the garden where your body has been resting, refreshing, and healing," I heard Dr. Weiss say.

I was no longer watching the body of a dying woman in her bed. I was returning to the present time. My mind was reconnecting with my body.

"And now it is time to awaken," Dr. Weiss said calmly. "I will awaken you by counting up from one to ten. When I say ten you can open your eyes. You will be awake and alert, in full control of your body and your mind. Feeling wonderful, refreshed, relaxed, filled with beautiful energy. Feeling great. One . . . two . . . three . . . more awake and alert, feeling wonderful . . . four . . . five . . . six, more and more awake, feeling great . . . seven . . . eight . . . nearly awake now . . . nine . . . ten."

On the count of ten, I opened my eyes and was surprised to find that my cheeks were wet with tears. I felt calm, yet energized. What had just happened? The experience was so real. I was in awe.

It was time to break for lunch. In a nearby restaurant, Tracey and I sat across from each other, sharing our morning experiences. I began telling Tracey about my first memory of being in a carriage as a child.

"Wait!" Tracey said. "I was in that carriage with you. I saw you!"

She began describing to me what she saw during her past-life memory, which was eerily similar to mine, right down to the description of my father and the puddle outside the carriage. Could Tracey have been the other girl with me in the carriage, the girl I thought to be my sister or cousin? This was becoming more and more interesting.

Chapter 4: A Gift from My Grandmother

Our lunch break was coming to an end, and while Tracey excused herself, I sat at the table reviewing the workshop agenda. The morning had been spent discovering extraordinary details about past lives. According to the agenda, the afternoon was to be spent discovering new tools for developing intuition and psychic abilities. I bit my lip as I continued reading. "*This exciting experiential workshop takes you on an incredible psycho-spiritual journey as you explore the limitless boundaries of the mind and soul.*"

I had experienced psycho-spiritual journeys and knew how intense they could be. I closed my eyes and took a deep breath. I recalled my husband's words from the other night:

"Well, how do you explain what happened when your grandmother died?"

I thought back to 2006. Although my grandmother had suffered a stroke and could no longer speak, I knew she heard every word I said. She would squeeze my hand in response to conversation. Her eyes would fill with tears as I shared memories of the past. I remembered being so upset to learn that no one had told her why she was first brought to the hospital. Although she was non-verbal, I could see in her eyes that she was scared and confused. I crawled into the hospital bed with her and took her hand. I looked her in the eyes and explained that she had a stroke. I explained what the doctors were doing and kept her in the medical loop.

It was obvious how uncomfortable others were when they came to visit my grandmother. They appeared awkward, not knowing what to say or how to act. Visitors would speak to each other and not to my grandmother. The only other person who felt comfortable talking with and holding my grandmother was my younger sister.

After my grandmother was moved from the hospital to hospice, my sister and I spent our days reading and talking to her. We held her hands, massaged lotion on her skin, and crawled in bed to snuggle with her. I never felt closer to my grandmother or my sister than I did then.

I had returned home one day about eight p.m. after spending the day at hospice. I sat down in the recliner, put my feet up and turned on the television. Suddenly, I felt a strong presence and knew I was not alone. I turned my head to my left and saw a man standing in the corner of the room. He was short and was dressed in a three-piece suit from the 1930s. He wore a Fedora. He looked at me solemnly and nodded. He telepathically communicated to me that my grandmother's time had come and she would be leaving soon. He assured me that he would guide her to the other side. With another nod of his head, he was gone.

While it was clear that this man knew my grandmother, I had never seen him before and did not know who he was.

"Mom, mom, are you okay?" It was my teenage son, Michael. I don't know how long he had been in the room, but there he was standing beside me.

"Did you see him?" I asked my son with urgency.

"See who?" Michael responded.

"The man. The man who was just standing over there, in the corner of the room. The man who nodded to me and told me that Grandma's time had come and that he would be waiting for her. The man in the hat. Did you see him? He was right there!"

My son had not seen him, but he believed that I had seen him.

The next day when I arrived at hospice to see my grandmother, my uncle was in the room with her. He had a box of miscellaneous items with him.

"I'm glad to see you," he said to me. "I have some things here that I found in your grandmother's attic that I think may interest you."

There, among the items was a scrapbook filled with my grandmother's precious memorabilia. I immediately began browsing through the pages. As I turned a page, I let out a gasp. There he was — the man who had visited me the night before. In the photo, he was wearing the same suit and Fedora that I had seen last night. Surrounding his picture were Ann Landers articles that my grandmother had cut out from various newspapers. Each advice column dealt with the same subject matter: fatherhood. Could this man be my grandmother's father?

I asked my uncle who the man in the picture was. He told me it was my grandmother's biological father. My great grandmother, whom I had known, became pregnant with my grandmother at a young age, but the father did not stick around to help raise his child or play the part of a family man.

I learned so much about my grandmother that day. I carefully read each Ann Landers column, which she had painstakingly clipped from the newspaper and meticulously placed in her scrapbook. Each column dealt with a reader asking for advice about fathers, about finding fathers who had never been a part of their child's life, advice about mending a broken heart.

My grandmother also had collected poems, stories, and articles about fatherhood. She had paid homage to a man she did not know, a man whose image haunted her throughout her life. I had heard through the family that at some point my grandmother did track down her biological father. I don't know if she met him, but she did have contact with him. To help relieve his guilt, he gave my grandmother some money, which she used to update her kitchen.

This man had given me a valuable gift to share with my grandmother. Revealing himself to me dressed exactly as he was in the photo gave me the verification I needed. He was the biological father that my grandmother had been mourning throughout her life.

That evening while I was alone with my grandmother, we looked through the scrapbook together. I read some of the poems and articles to her. I showed her pictures. And I told her about my visitor. I assured her that the father she so desperately sought in this life was waiting for her in the next. He would be there to cross her over. A tear fell from her eye and ran down her cheek. I put on some soft music, curled up in bed with my grandma and just held her. I felt closer to her and understood her more in that moment than I ever had.

Later that evening, as other family members returned to be with my grandmother, I decided to take a break. I drove home with a feeling of calm and peace. I arrived home looking forward to some much-needed rest. I had just stepped out of the shower when the phone rang. It was my sister. "The hospice nurse said grandma will not be here much longer. She won't make it through the night."

"I'm on my way." I quickly threw on clothes and rushed back to the hospital.

I didn't make it in time. She had taken her last breath moments before I returned. I stood by her bed, holding her hand, looking at the body that once housed the spirit of my grandmother. She had been a beautiful lady. The rest of the family did not remain long. Soon, it was just me and my sister left in the room with my grandmother. My sister and I continued to hold my grandmother's hands and to speak lovingly to her. My grandmother was known for wearing bright red lipstick. I gently put some red lipstick on her pale, dry lips. Within minutes my sister said, "Look!"

We both watched as my grandmother's eyes opened and regained their crystal, sparkling appearance. We watched as her pale, sallow skin became vibrant with a rose blush in her cheeks. A smile crossed her face.

No, her body did not come back to life. Her spirit had left her body, which was no longer able to serve her. Her smile was her gift to her two granddaughters who loved her through to her next life. She was letting us know she had made it to the other side. She was at peace. She was thankful.

Was I a freak as my husband claimed? The fear of that label had prevented me from accepting and sharing my experiences in the past, but I was about to get a strong reminder of what it feels like to receive a visitor from the other side.

"Are you ready for round two?' Tracey asked as she gathered her belongings from our lunch table.

"I'm ready," I said as I pushed in my chair. As we headed back to the convention center, I heard a voice within whisper, "Yes. You *are* ready."

Chapter 5: A Message from Beyond

We returned to the convention center and took our seats. Dr. Weiss instructed us to partner with someone we did not know. Tracey and I approached two women in front of us. I held out my hand and introduced myself to my partner. She reluctantly placed her wizened hand in mine. Her nebulous eyes showed her fatigue, and her glasses didn't hide the deep creases under them.

Dr. Weiss told partners to sit across from each other. Each person was to hand the other a personal item. I took off my diamond engagement ring and placed it in my partner's creased palm. She let out a sigh and with exasperation asked, "Is any of this working for you?"

I hesitated and said, "Actually, yes. Yes, it is. I had a pretty remarkable experience during the morning exercise. How about you? Is this working for you?"

"No," she said. "Not at all. It's a waste of time, and I'm ready to leave. This isn't for me. I shouldn't be here."

Her tone was brittle and exasperated. I watched as she placed my ring in her lap and used her desiccated fingers to reluctantly rummage through her purse. She randomly withdrew an object that resembled a plastic piece to a cell phone and handed it to me.

She shrugged and said, "I have nothing to give you. It doesn't matter anyway."

I took the plastic piece and held it in my hand. Dr. Weiss dimmed the lights and told us all to close our eyes and place the object our partner had given us against our solar plexus. He instructed us to just allow whatever entered our mind to flow and not try to figure it out or question it.

I sat with my eyes closed, holding the plastic item to my solar plexus, relaxed and breathing deeply. I listened to Dr. Weiss' calm voice and the soothing background music. Soon, my mind took me on another journey. I saw a much younger version of my partner standing over the stove in the kitchen of a row house, stirring a large pot of stew or soup. In the background were children's voices laughing, talking, and squealing. I could feel that cooking for these children was very important to my partner and something that she held dear to her heart. I knew she was caring for these children, and most of them were not her own. Suddenly, a very strong, white light cleared the image of the woman cooking. Coming out of the light was a man. He was a soldier in a green uniform. He was carrying a large bouquet of beautiful wild flowers. I was overcome with a warm feeling of love.

The soldier began to communicate with me. He expressed the urgency of getting his message to my partner. I needed to tell her the flowers were for her, but not to worry, he picked them himself because he knew how she does not agree with spending money on flowers. He wished he had given her more flowers and not listened to her objections. He said to please tell her that he is well and that although the two of them were reserved in showing affection and were not publicly demonstrative, he loved her deeply and still does. He instructed that I had to make it clear to her that it was not her time yet and that she needed to be strong. He was fine and would be waiting for her, but until then, she was to live life, knowing that he was still with her and loved her dearly.

Dr. Weiss' voice was now bringing us out of this altered state. I opened my eyes, still feeling the warmth of the love that this soldier had brought to me. Dr. Weiss told us to share with our partners all images and experiences that came to us. He told us not to judge or question, just share.

My partner had my ring in her hand. She shook her head and said she felt and saw nothing at all.

"I am sorry," she said. "This just isn't working for me." She handed me my ring and lowered her head.

It was my turn. I looked at the woman who sat across from me. She appeared to be disinterested and wanting to leave. I cleared my throat and began by saying, "I don't know if any of this will make sense to you, but I'll relay what I experienced and take it from there."

I proceeded to tell her everything, starting with my vision of her cooking in the kitchen with a house full of children and ending with the message given to me by the soldier. I stopped talking, took a breath and looked at my partner. She was sitting across from me, staring, not saying a word. No confirmation. No reaction. Tracey's partner, the younger woman who was with my partner, had been listening to me as well.

With a shocked look of disbelief, the younger woman asked, "Can you please repeat what you said?"

"Sure," I answered and shared my experiences again. This time a tear rolled down my partner's cheek. Tracey's partner lovingly put her arm around my partner. "That's her husband! She's been waiting for a sign from him. He passed away six weeks ago. She came here hoping for some kind of message from him."

My partner looked at me and spoke.

"Are you a psychic?" she asked me.

"Well, no, not really," I stammered.

"Everything you said to me is true. I used to cook for the children in our neighborhood. It was hard times, and I would bring the neighborhood children to my home. I would teach them. I would cook large pots of stew and soup and feed them. My husband was a soldier. He knew how I felt about wasting money, which is why I told him never to buy me flowers. That's why he told you to make sure I knew that he picked them. I've been looking and waiting to hear from him. I have gone to psychics and have gotten no results. This was my last hope. I was going to stop searching after this."

This woman, my partner, got up from her seat. She stood in front of me and put her arms around me, embracing me in a tight hug. She whispered in my ear. Her voice was quivering.

"You saved my life," she said. "I was going to end my life tonight if I didn't hear from him today. I miss him so. I'll now be able to go on. I'll wait. You saved my life."

Once the embrace was over, my partner and I took a long look at each other. Her appearance had changed, softened. The cloudy look of her eyes was replaced with a twinkle. Her demeanor of despair had been replaced with relief and hope.

It was at that moment I knew. I had reached a turning point in my life. I wasn't able to define it, but I felt it. I knew that all I had experienced at this workshop had deep meaning. I couldn't ignore it. I also knew that by embracing this experience my life would never be the same.

Chapter 6: Unlocking Doors to the Past

A few weeks had passed since the workshop, and I no longer felt the need to jump back on the treadmill life I had created. Better yet, I no longer wanted to jump back on that treadmill. I felt as though I had entered a new dimension.

"Aren't you getting up and going to the school?" I heard my husband ask me as I rolled over and looked at the alarm clock glaring at me on the nightstand. I pulled the covers up to my chin and closed my eyes.

"No, you go in without me. I'm not feeling too well this morning. If anyone needs anything or has any questions, they can call me at home."

My husband pulled up the shades, and I felt the March sun stream through the window, hitting my cheek. "Okay," my husband replied as he disappeared into the bathroom.

I lay in bed and stretched, stared at the ceiling and realized that my interest in working at the school had diminished since Dr. Weiss' workshop. After seeing another life and being told that I had saved a life, how could I return to the life I knew? There were now other things that captured my interest. Mysteries to solve. Secrets to reveal. A new journey waiting to unfold.

Once my husband left and I got my daughter off to school, I took the CD I had bought from Dr. Weiss' workshop and placed it in the CD player. I lay on the couch, closed my eyes and waited for Dr. Weiss' gentle voice to guide me through a regression.

"Go back into your childhood and recall a pleasant memory," instructed Dr. Weiss. His voice on the CD was a bit rushed and not quite as soothing as it was during the seminar, but I soon found myself transported to an altered state of relaxation and another era.

The tips of my shoes were the only thing peaking out from behind the drapes. It was all I could do to stifle my giggles as Mammy stormed around the house looking for me. "You know it's time for your lessons. You can't hide from me forever."

Education was taken seriously in our home, and I was farther ahead in my studies than most young girls my age. However, the thought of sitting still and serious for such a long time made me want to run and have a bit of fun before I began my lessons.

I soon heard Mammy's footsteps in the dining room, where I was hiding behind the drapes.

"Now who do you suppose left these shoes here behind these drapes?" Mammy said. I put my hand over my mouth and bit my tongue to keep from laughing out loud. "I know I've told these children not to leave their things lying around the house."

As soon as she finished her sentence, her large, rough, dark hand pulled back the drapes to expose me standing there laughing in hysterics. No matter how many times I played this hide-and-seek game with Mammy, I was always amused by it.

"Lordy, child! I don't know why you insist on hiding when you know it's time for your lessons. The governess is waiting for you, and you know how she does not like to wait! Now hurry!"

With a smile on my face, I skipped out of the dining room and headed off to do my schoolwork with the governess.

My memory was interrupted by Dr. Weiss' voice.

"If you wish to go further, we can do that now," he gently suggested. "Go to significant events. Spend as much time as you need and find the answers."

I watched as a young girl in the late 19th century floated in the air, moving ahead in time. When she landed she was a young woman.

The large mansion was brightly lit and sent a warm glow into the evening darkness. I looked out the window and watched as guests dressed in formal attire descended from carriages and ascended the stairs to the mansion. This was a festive occasion. We were celebrating the engagement of my sister. I should have been happy, but I was not. Was it because I was the eldest daughter and should be the first to marry? No. I was not interested in marriage. I just knew in my heart that my sister was not truly happy with her decision to marry. She appeared happy, but I struggled to believe it. I struggled to accept it. I struggled over the feeling that I had lost her, the sister I had helped raise, whom I had expected to stay with me forever. We would teach school together, live together, grow old together. She was getting married. She was leaving me. I was the one who was not truly happy with her decision.

I looked over the railing from the third floor of the house and watched as the guests entered the hallway. I decided to regain control of my feelings and join the party. I descended the stairs and entered the large main rooms of the house.

The rooms were bright, festive, and alive with the affluent people of our city. Elegantly dressed people mingled and drank while the servants attended to their needs by taking coats and wraps from the arriving guests, passing silver platters of hors d'oeuvres, and making sure glasses of spirit were never empty.

I painted a smile on my face, nodded and made small talk with some of the guests. Then I saw him from across the room. My sister's fiancé. Yes, we grew up together, and he was a nice enough man, but not for my sister. Arranged marriages did not feel right to me. Keeping things within the family did not feel right to me. I would never allow that for myself, and it was hard for me to accept that my sister would allow it for herself. She said she loved him. That was not my worry. Did he love her and could he be faithful? That was where my doubt lay.

My eyes filled with tears, and I was suddenly taken over by a wave of heat. I felt flushed. I turned to exit the room, only to bump into my sister who was standing behind me. Our eyes met, and she saw the tears falling down my cheeks. I lowered my head and quickly walked into the hallway and out the front door. By this time I was running. I ran across the street and into the square. I took a deep breath and inhaled the sweet smell of magnolias and Spanish moss while the coolness of the night air soothed my emotion.

As I stood in the square, I turned to face the house I had just left. The illumination from the windows made the house glow brilliantly and look as if it was the only home alive on the square. I watched as the large front door to the home opened and my sister appeared on the porch, looking for me. I couldn't face her. I did not want to. Things would never be the same. Soon the door to the house opened again, and I saw my sister's fiancé standing on the porch. He was consoling my sister. He put his arm around her shoulders. He was persuading her to come back in the house, to join the party, not to worry about me. Reluctantly, my sister agreed. I watched from the square as my sister and her husband-to-be walked into the house and closed the door. I walked through the square and looked down the road to see the beautiful fountain in the park. I was tempted to walk to the fountain, but I knew in my heart that I needed to go back to the party.

"And now it is time to awaken," Dr. Weiss' voice said.

No, it can't be time already, I thought. Just a few minutes more, please!

"I will awaken you by counting up from one to ten. When I say ten, you can open your eyes."

My eyes opened wide at the count of ten, and I quickly sat up, gasping. The fountain! I knew where that fountain was! It was the fountain in Forsyth Park, Savannah. My regressions were taking place in Savannah, Georgia! Things were starting to click, and my story was unfolding.

Chapter 7: Welcome Home

Belief is not merely an idea that the mind possesses; it is an idea that possesses the mind. —Playwright and Screenwriter Robert Bolt (1924–1995)

Savannah introduced itself to me in this lifetime through the movies. In the late 1990s, my husband owned a video store. On the weekends, he would bring home a movie for us to watch after we put Michael to bed. On one particular evening, my husband brought home Midnight in the Garden of Good and Evil. I hadn't read John Berendt's book and knew nothing of the story.

"What's this movie about?" I asked Mark.

"I'm not quite sure, but it's supposed to be good," he said.

I made the popcorn, poured the drinks, dimmed the lights and settled on the couch next to Mark. We weren't more than five or ten minutes into the movie when I got an overwhelming feeling of recognition. I turned to my husband and said, "I've been there before. I recognize the scenery."

He looked at me strangely.

"Well, maybe you were there as a child, but I don't ever remember you talking about going to Savannah, and I know we've never been there."

"Savannah? This movie is taking place in Savannah, Georgia?" I thought a moment. "I've never been to Savannah, but the streets, building, and scenery are all very familiar to me."

I continued to watch the movie, spellbound, not by the plot but by the setting. I could see myself walking down the brick streets, lined with beautiful old oak trees dripping with Spanish moss. I could feel the warm Savannah air against my cheek and smell the sweet aroma of azaleas as they bloomed in the city squares. I recognized the haunting beauty, the dirt roads and the gothic statues of Bonaventure cemetery, which was featured in the film. I don't know how much attention I actually paid to the storyline, but I knew I would always remember the feeling that came over me while watching Midnight in the Garden of Good Evil. I felt as if I had gone home.

Life continued after that. I soon put aside any thoughts of Savannah. I chased my aspirations of success and acceptance by working full time, attending graduate school, caring for my son, maintaining a home, and tending to daily life.

I didn't encounter Savannah again until 2001, when friends of ours chose Savannah as a meeting point to enjoy a long weekend together. We had been very close to the two couples we were meeting and had not seen either couple since they moved south a few years earlier. One of our friends who joined us for this reunion had been to Savannah on business. She was familiar with the city and made arrangements for us to stay at the Eliza Thompson House, a bed and breakfast that was one of her favorites. I was excited to catch up with my friends, spend some time with my husband and celebrate my accomplishments.

The plane landed at the Savannah airport, and we took a cab to the historic city. The minute the cab turned onto Jones Street I had the same familiar feeling I had experienced while watching Midnight in the Garden of Good and Evil. Soon the cab came to a stop in front of the Eliza Thompson House. As I stepped onto the brick-paved street, lined with massive oak trees that dangled Spanish moss over my head like a protective canopy, I was overcome with a sense of having been here before. In my mind I saw myself on this very street wearing Victorian style clothes, nodding to others as they passed in their horse-drawn carriages.

The cab left, and I continued to stand in front of the Eliza Thompson House, gazing at the exquisite 1847 home. The front porch leading to the entrance of the bed and breakfast was flanked with twin staircases, one for the ladies and one for the gentlemen. Before ascending the stairs, I inhaled the Savannah air, capturing the recognizable sweet, fruity, fragrance of magnolia that I had experienced while watching Midnight in the Garden of Good and Evil. My mind told me that I had never traveled to Savannah before, but my heart and senses told me otherwise. Somewhere deep down I knew that this trip to this gorgeous city was not my first.

As much as I tried to shake it off, the plaguing sense of familiarity would not leave. One day I went shopping with the other woman with us on the trip. We decided to walk from The Eliza Thompson and head towards the river. The weather was cool, the sky clear, and there was no lull in conversation as we covered the years since we had last seen each other.

The city of Savannah was alive with tourists bearing cameras around their necks, viewing the city from tour buses and trolleys. Students from Savannah College of Art and Design were cycling throughout the city, immersed in community projects, while Savannah residents strolled the streets with their leashed dogs in hand. We walked and marveled at the squares, lined with elegant, restored homes that preserved the uniqueness and history of this city with its 18th-, 19th-, and early 20th-century architecture. What started as a pleasant walk, enjoying the company of old friends and the scenery of the city, soon took a turn. I began to feel anxious and uncomfortable. The farther we walked from Jones Street and the closer we got to the river, the worse I felt. I heard a quiet, yet stern, voice somewhere within me say, "You know you shouldn't be in this part of the city. It is not proper."

I looked at the other women with me, laughing, chatting and walking through the city. They seemed to be enjoying themselves, unaware of any change in the atmosphere. I couldn't understand my discomfort. I shook my head, discounted the inner voice and wrote off the feeling as being overtired.

Historic River Street, paved with 200-year-old cobblestones, runs along the Savannah River and is glittered with century-old warehouses that were once home for stored cotton. These buildings have now been converted to unique art galleries, eclectic antique shops, quaint pubs, fabulous restaurants, and magnificent hotels. When we arrived at the river my heart raced. It was wider than I had imagined. The turbid brown water flowed swiftly and strongly, carrying decades of secrets and hiding a myriad of dangers in its swift undertow. The March wind from the water left me chilled, and I found myself wrapping my coat closer to my body, trying to hide my shivering bones. The street was full with tourists buying souvenirs, tangible items to remind them of this moment. As we meandered through the crowds, I was remembering a time when this port was crowded with merchants, factories, and traders conducting their business from the decks of ships and the wharves along the river.

We reached the end of the river walk and headed south towards Broughton Street. There we immediately began exploring the shops that adorned both sides of the street. Inside the warehouse that is home to Paris Market, we each went on a separate journey to discover the treasures uniquely displayed throughout the two floors of the store. Some of my anxiety eased among the home furnishings and Parisian treasures, but as soon as I stepped outside onto the sidewalk, the inner voice returned.

"You need to get back home. This is no place for a lady," the voice said.

"Hey, are you alright?" my friend asked me with a bit of concern in her voice.

"Yeah, I'm okay," I said. "I'm just feeling a bit tired and out of sorts."

"Let's start heading back to the bed and breakfast," another friend suggested. "This way we can relax and have a glass of wine in the parlor before we all go out for dinner."

"Sounds like a great idea," I said.

The four of us began walking back in the direction of the bed and breakfast, located in the residential section on affluent Jones Street. With each step I took away from Broughton Street I could feel my anxiety decrease. It wasn't until we passed Chippewa Square and approached Madison Square that my uneasiness was replaced with a wave of relief that shot from my head to my toes, wrapping my body in a blanket of calm. My inner voice sighed, relieved that I was back home.

During this first visit to Savannah, I toured the home of Juliette Gordon Lowe, founder of the Girl Scouts, saw the bench where the fictional Forrest Gump sat, enjoyed the beauty of the fountain in Forsyth Park, took a ghost tour, and dined at the Pink House. I learned from the ghost tour the history of Broughton Street and the Riverfront. This area was where men would conduct business, pirates would dine, "ladies of the night" entertained customers, gamblers collected debts, slaves were shackled, and true women did not set foot. This would explain why a woman from centuries past would have felt uncomfortable in this area. But why was I so ill at ease in that part of the city?

Throughout my stay, I continued to feel as though I had been to this city before. It was in the historic Pink House during dinner that I was overcome with a strong feeling of love and recognition. Sitting at a table in the upstairs dining area, a warm tingling sensation swept through my body, and the familiar smell of my grandmother engulfed my senses. I felt wrapped in the warm glow of love as a voice inside said, "Welcome home."

Chapter 8: The House

Old houses tell a story. They have a history. There is something about running your hand down a banister that generations of people have held in their hands for centuries. It gives you a sense of place and time, and a perspective on where you fit in this huge, sometimes impersonal world. You are a part — a small but important part — of a much greater story.— Scott Austin Sidler, PreservationNation Blog

April 2010 came quickly. It had been nearly two months since the Dr. Weiss workshop, and my desire to solve the mystery of my regressions had grown. I had been sharing these memories with Tracey, who was also curious to explain her own experiences. Tracey's regressions were strangely similar to mine, and she was convinced that we had been together during a past life in Savannah. We made up our minds that we needed to go to Savannah to find the missing pieces.

April brought spring break, which meant a ten-day vacation from school and work. Instead of using this time as I usually did, to catch up on work and plan for the school's summer program, Tracey and I made plans for our families to return to Savannah. It had been nine years since my first visit, and I wanted to know if my past life regressions were connected to my familiarity with Savannah during that trip. We wanted to see if anything would validate our memories. Once again, we made reservations at the Eliza Thompson House, purchased tickets for the Home and Garden tour, and counted down the days until we left.

My husband, daughter, and I arrived in Savannah a day before Tracey and her husband. As soon as we entered the historic district,

I had, as in my first visit, that eerie feeling that I was once again home. It was later in the evening by the time we arrived on Jones Street and settled into our room. Although it was dark outside, I grabbed my daughter and husband by the hands and said, "Let's go for a walk!"

"Are you crazy?" my husband asked. "It's late. We'll do plenty of walking tomorrow!"

"I just want to take a quick walk. It won't be long. I need to inhale the Savannah air, and I'm eager to explore."

With that, Jennifer happily obliged while Mark shook his head and followed us out the door. I immediately turned right onto Jones Street and made another right heading towards Monterey Square, home of the Mercer house, which played a starring role in Midnight in the Garden of Good and Evil. I felt pulled in this direction by an unknown force. The evening breeze was cool as it ran through my hair, kissed my cheek and pushed me closer to my destination.

In the square I stopped suddenly. I inhaled deeply, holding my breath, not believing what I saw standing in front of me. There, on the corner of Bull Street and Gordon, in Monterey Square, in all its grandeur, was an Italianate style mansion, with a cast-iron balcony and gold painted on the outer frames of the window. My eyes wandered to the top of the mansion, taking in the wonderful cupola that offered a 360-degree view of Savannah. It was almost exactly the way I saw it in my regression, although the color of stucco appeared to have changed from gray to pink over the years. This was *The House.* It was the mansion where my sister had her engagement party. It was where I had run down the front stairs to escape into the square in which I was currently standing.

As I stood in the square and looked down Bull Street, I saw the fountain in the distance. The fountain in Forsyth Park. The huge, white, ornate, two-tiered structure of cast iron with the figure of a woman at the top stood glowing in its nighttime spotlight. It was the fountain I had seen in my regression. The fountain that made me realize my regressions were taking place in Savannah. The fountain had brought me back home.

I stood there, dumbstruck.

"Mom, what's wrong?" I heard Jennifer ask as she stood next to me, pulling my hand. "Why did you stop?"

Without taking my eyes off the mansion, I answered, "Nothing's wrong, honey. I'm just taking in the beauty of this huge house."

I continued holding Jennifer's hand and moved across the street until I was standing on the sidewalk, directly in front of the mansion. I noted the wrought iron fencing around the home, something that was not present during my regression. I allowed my eyes to gaze upward, and I saw that some windows in what appeared to be the attic level were broken. I had no doubt that this was the house I had seen in my dreamlike state as Dr. Weiss' voice opened doors to my memory.

My husband was soon behind me. I reached out and grabbed his hand.

"This is it," I whispered. "This is the house. The house I've seen in my regression. This is it! I need to get inside. I need to see if the inside of the home is the way I saw it. The way I experienced it."

My husband kissed my head, and in a silence of disbelief and overwhelming excitement, we walked back to the Eliza Thompson.

Tracey and Paul would be arriving late tomorrow afternoon. I would not say a word to her about the house. Tracey claimed to have seen the same house during one of her regressions. I would wait to see if she found it on her own.

The next morning, after a leisurely breakfast in the courtyard of the Eliza Thompson, we decided to spend the day being tourists. Tracey and her husband would not arrive until dinner. Until then, my husband, Jennifer and I were on our own to tour the historic district in a horse and carriage, visit River Street Sweets candy store, have lunch at the Gryphon Tea Room, and explore the gift shops in City Market.

We met Tracey and Paul for dinner at an Italian restaurant on Broughton Street. I was careful not to mention my discovery of the mansion. We had tickets to tour the Mercer house during our stay, so I knew Tracey and I would be going to Monterey Square. I knew we would be walking by the mansion. I was going to wait and see if she had any reaction to the house.

After dinner we leisurely walked back in the direction of the Eliza Thompson House, taking in the beauty, architecture, and history of the city. We stopped for dessert and coffee at Gallery Espresso, which was filled with the diverse culture of the city. College students sat in groups, gathered around laptops, sipping flavored coffee while brainstorming their next projects, and tourists foraged through maps and brochures with their cappuccinos cooling on the table. We found a quiet corner that consisted of two large, mismatched, wingback chairs and an overstuffed maroon sofa, where we sat and ate our dessert. We transferred our drinks to travel cups so we could continue to walk and enjoy the sights. As we approached Jones Street, I noticed Tracey's pace quicken. Once we reached Jones Street, instead of turning to go to the Eliza Thompson, Tracey kept walking. Her pace continued to increase, and I grabbed Jennifer's hand, struggling to keep up with Tracey. She was soon quite a distance ahead of us, and Paul called to me, "Where is she going?"

I didn't answer, but I knew. Tracey was being drawn to the mansion. The same way I had been drawn there the night before.

By the time Jennifer and I caught up to Tracey, she was standing in Monterey Square, on the sidewalk, directly in front of the mansion. I stood quietly next to her.

"This is it!" Tracey declared. "It's the house I saw in the regression."

"I know!" I answered breathlessly. "I was brought to it last night, when we arrived. I was waiting to see if you would discover it, too."

"There's something different about the house, though," Tracey said. "The iron railings were not in the front yard during my regression. They must have been added later, but everything else is the same."

That was confirmation to me that we had seen the same house. I couldn't believe it. Tracey had found the house. She found it her first night in Savannah, as I did. She had been pulled to it, as I was.

I knew then that there was something to these memories that were being brought to the surface. Some force was leading me to this moment. But why? Everything seemed so surreal.

The next day we had tickets for the Home and Garden Tour. We spent the day touring lavishly restored historic homes and gardens throughout the city. We roamed through homes built during the height of the Cotton Era that proudly displayed architectural elements of the 19th-century Romantic Revival. We strolled broad brick-paved streets with elegant row houses canopied by huge oaks. We wandered through courtyards protected by wrought-iron gates. In their gardens, the potpourri of scents registered as a sweet mix of jasmine, grass, and blossoms. As much as Tracey and I appreciated the tour, the only home on our minds was our mansion, which unfortunately was not part of the agenda.

That evening, we had dinner reservations at Elizabeth on 37th. The restaurant was not within walking distance from the Eliza Thompson House, so we drove our rental car to the heart of the Victorian District. The grayish coloring of the 20th-century mansion, once home to a cotton broker, cast a strange glow as we walked through a fragrant herb garden leading to the restaurant's entrance.

We climbed the steps to the columned front porch and slowly opened the large, wooden doors into the lobby. The historic colors and patterns on the walls, the fresh flowers on antique tables and the original paintings and ceramics took me back in time. I gladly embraced my immersion in old-world Southern hospitality.

Jennifer and her American Girl doll entertained themselves with coloring books and crayons while the adults enjoyed a relaxing evening of sumptuous food and conversation. Tracey's husband was a skeptic, so we didn't spend much time discussing our past life experiences or the house. Once we were completely satiated with half moon river clams, spicy Savannah red rice with Georgia shrimp, pepper crusted beef tenderloin, and chocolate pecan torte, we rolled out of Elizabeth on 37th and headed back to the Eliza Thompson. Jennifer fought to keep her eyes open during the short drive back to the inn. My body was tired, but my mind was keeping it awake with the many questions running through my head.

By the time I tucked Jennifer into bed, gently kissing her forehead, Mark was already snoring in the bed next to her. I took off my shoes, allowing my toes to wriggle and giving my feet a chance to breathe. I was about to undress when there was a knock on our door.

"I can't sleep now," Tracey said as I opened the door to our room. She was wearing sneakers and a jacket, prepared to go outside. I quickly put my shoes back on my tired feet and quietly closed the door behind me.

The night air was cool, and I wrapped my long sweater closer to my body searching for warmth against the unusually cold breeze that seemed to be pushing me to my destination. Once we reached the square, Tracey and I sat on a bench, staring at the stately mansion, illuminated by the streetlight and small lamp glowing in the downstairs window. As I gazed at the magnificent building, I wondered, who lives in this house now? Would it look as it did in my regression? I slowly got up and approached the building. I stood on the sidewalk, getting as close to the home as possible without standing on the porch. I closed my eyes and recalled the glory in which I first saw this home. It was the late 1800s. The mansion was beautifully illuminated with light in each window and alive with the finest people in the city of Savannah.

I opened my eyes to find Tracey standing next to me, intently examining the home.

"I believe I was the girl having the engagement party in your regression," Tracey quietly stated, without taking her eyes off the mansion. "In my regression, I saw you run down these stairs. I saw you turn this corner."

As she relived her memory, we walked to the corner of the house, where she saw me turn in her regression. It was the corner of Bull Street. As we reached the corner, my eyes wandered to the fountain in Forsyth Park, clearly visible. Tracey was drawn to something else.

"Look over here!" she said. "There's a sign on the side of the house."

We stood on the corner of Gordon Street and Bull. My eyes focused where Tracey was pointing. The lower basement level of the home had an entrance on Bull Street. There above the entrance was a sign that read "Alex Raskin Antiques."

"The lower level of the home must be an antique shop," Tracey exclaimed.

We approached the side entrance, and I peered into the window of the antique shop's door. In the darkened interior I could see an old wooden cradle and an oak cane-backed wheelchair resting near the entrance. The walls were stacked from floor to ceiling with writing desks, chairs, crystal candleholders, gilded mirrors, family portraits, books and any other antique imaginable. Spine-chilling excitement ran through my body as I soaked in the contents of this basement room.

We noted the hours of operation posted in the windowpane of the door: 10 a.m. to 5 p.m. Tracey and I turned to look at each other. We both knew where we would be tomorrow at 10 a.m.

It was all we could do to contain ourselves through breakfast the next morning. Time seemed to stand still while we sat at the wrought-iron table in the classic courtyard of the Eliza Thompson, picking at our food. Eating breakfast was usually relaxing, with the soft, splashing sounds of the koi pond and water sculptures adding to the intimacy of this garden paradise. This morning was different. I poured myself another cup of coffee, and Tracey helped herself to more fruit to fill time while we awaited our departure.

I watched Jennifer as she followed Virginia, the inn's cook, from the kitchen into the courtyard, breakfast in hand. Jennifer had been drawn to the large, friendly, dark-skinned woman from the first moment she saw Virginia carrying trays of breakfast food into the courtyard for the wakening guests. During our first morning breakfast, Jennifer complimented Virginia on her cooking and automatically began to help her clear the dirty dishes. She and Jennifer had formed a close friendship during our stay, and Virginia made it a point to bring Jennifer to the kitchen each morning to make her a special breakfast. Jennifer brought her plate, piled with a fluffy omelet, grits, bacon, and toast, to the table and sat next to me. I watched as she eagerly ate her food, enjoying every bite of it. When Virginia emerged from the kitchen again, Jennifer ran to her with open arms, embracing her tightly as she thanked her for the meal.

"It's 9:50," Tracey announced as she tapped me on the shoulder. Her short stature, small frame, and sparkling jewelry made Tracey appear almost fairy-like as she floated through the garden, saying her goodbyes to our families.

I obediently gulped down the last of my coffee, grabbed my purse and stood to leave.

"We are going to *The House,*" I said as I leaned over to kiss my husband good-bye. "We'll be exploring the antique shop in the lower level, and hopefully someone working there can give us some information about the building."

I kissed Jennifer silently on the cheek and gave her a tight squeeze.

"You and Daddy will meet us at the house when he's finished with his breakfast."

She and her American Girl doll were busy assigning names to the koi in the pond and didn't take much notice of me leaving.

She looked up long enough to say, "Okay, Mommy!" and went right back to naming the fish.

Tracey and I walked briskly, practically holding our breath with anticipation. We arrived at the side entrance to the lower level on Bull Street. I waited for what seemed a lifetime as Tracey opened the door to the antique shop. As soon as we stepped inside, we were hit with a strong smell that was a combination of must, dust, mold, and the lingering aroma of years gone by. The rooms were filled with antiques of all shapes, sizes, and time periods. As we slowly maneuvered our way through a path of old furniture, I saw a young woman peer from around a counter, offering a big smile in our direction.

"Good morning!" she called to us. "Please let me know if I can help you with anything." She placed the last of her bagel in her mouth and washed it down with a swig of orange juice.

The college-age woman in jeans and a sweatshirt placed her juice container on the counter, sat on a stool and began sorting through a box of items.

"What a beautiful old home," I said as I approached her. She looked up and made eye contact with me.

"Yes. It's one of the only homes left that hasn't been restored or torn down," she said.

"Really?" I asked. "Do you know the history of this home?'

"Not much," she said. "All I know is what the owner, Mr. Raskin, has told me. The house is the Noble Hardee Mansion, named after its first owner, Noble Hardee. He was a cotton merchant who began building the home in 1860 but died before its completion. Throughout the Civil War, it remained unfinished until the Reconstruction era of the 1870s when it became one of the city's most sophisticated mansions. Mr. Raskin bought the home years ago, and it's home to his antiques. In addition to this level, we have three more levels of antiques in the main house."

My jaw dropped. "Three more levels?"

"Yes! Around the corner you'll find the staircase that leads to the main level. Feel free to explore all three additional levels, and if you need help or have any questions, come and get me. We just ask that you not enter the attic level. It's the only level off limits to customers because of safety issues and concerns."

The young woman pointed in the direction of the staircase, handed me a brochure and went back to rummaging through her box.

Tracey had been exploring the lower level of the house while I chatted with the clerk. I inched my way through the furniture, baby carriages, pictures, and books to find Tracey in a back room so crammed with antiques that we could barely turn around.

"Tracey!" I said, gasping. "We can go upstairs! This whole house is one big antique store! We can go upstairs and explore the whole house except the attic! The house hasn't been restored, and we can actually see the home. I can't believe this!" My hand was trembling with excitement as I took Tracey by the arm, leading her through the maze of clutter and back towards the main entrance.

As we left the back room, we heard the basement door open and the sound of our husbands' voices as they entered the store. Tracey and I greeted them giddily.

"Guess what?" I whispered. "We can go upstairs! We can go in the main house!"

My husband looked at me quizzically as I took his hand and led him to the staircase, followed by Jennifer, Tracey, and Paul. There it was, right in front of us. The staircase that would take me into the home I saw in my regression. This would determine whether what I saw was accurate. I stood in front of the stairs, afraid to take the first step up toward the main level. I vividly remembered everything I saw in my regression — the cream color of the walls, the amazingly high ceilings, the grand staircase that led to the two upper floors, the fireplaces, and the bedrooms on the third floor. I remembered myself peering over the railing at the guests who were entering the main hallway. I saw it. I felt it. Would walking through this home validate my vivid memories? Part of me was afraid to find out.

I slowly climbed the stairs, looking at all the antique photographs and posters that lined the staircase, hoping to find some clue. I made it to the top of the stairs and entered into the main house. As I turned and faced the main hallway leading to the front door of the home, my knees buckled and my hands began to shake. I held on tightly to my husband's arm for balance. As I stood with my back against the front door, gazing at the tremendous staircase flush with the wall to my right, I noticed a doorway prior to the staircase, leading to a side of the house I didn't recall. In my regression, the wall with the stairs was the end of the home. My eyes wandered to my left, and I saw beyond the peeling paint, the missing plaster on the walls and the rooms stuffed with antiques. What I saw to my left was what I had seen in my regression. I was able to describe each room prior to entering.

I took my husband by the hand. "This is it!" I said. "This is exactly how I remember it!"

Chapter 9: Opening a New Door

Eventually we will all understand that all wisdom is within us, and as we remember, practice and access this wisdom, we will become our own best teacher. — *Dr. Brian Weiss*

It had been a month since my trip to Savannah and the discovery of the house. The warm May sun had eliminated all evidence of the long, cold winter. I carefully balanced my mug of coffee and necessary school files while I opened the car door and gathered the strength to face another day. The bright, morning sun glared through the car windshield, and I put my hand in my purse, feeling for my sunglasses. As I put them on and started the car, I was tempted to drive in the direction of the beach instead of the school. My heart and mind were no longer focused on the school. They were in Savannah. They were thinking of the woman who so clearly came to me in my regressions and shared with me parts of her life. They were in the mansion sitting on Monterey Square. While I drove the familiar route to work, it dawned on me that much had transpired in the three months since I had attended Dr. Weiss' workshop.

Since then, my mind, body, and soul had craved something new. Exactly what that was, I wasn't sure yet. What I did know was that I needed meditation. The workshop forced me to do something I hadn't done since I was a child — quiet my mind. Sitting in a darkened room, with soft music playing in the background, and focusing on nothing but the guided meditation of Dr. Weiss' soothing voice refreshed me more than a week's vacation. Meditation was now something I wanted, or more appropriately, needed in my life.

I found myself going into work late so I could start my day with quiet mediation. Some meditations brought me messages, visions, or regressions. Other times I just grabbed a nice thirty-minute nap. No matter what the experience, after meditating, I felt refreshed, calm, and ready to face life with a new clarity.

This morning, after my husband had left for work and Jennifer had boarded the school bus, I had found myself sitting in the quiet of my family room, listening to the sounds of nature and taking deep breaths with my eyes gently closed. I cleared my mind and relaxed, while I inhaled deeply.

"It's time to let go," the voice said. "Your karma with the school is complete. Have faith. There are other experiences waiting for you. Let go. Move on. It's time."

I noticed that the more I meditated, the clearer the voice became. Tears flowed after hearing these words. The tears were not of sorrow, but of relief. I was waiting to be told it was okay. It was okay to say I needed to change. It was okay to let go. In some way, getting permission to let go of the school felt as though I was getting permission to let go of my ego and embrace the spirituality of life. It was giving me permission to take care of me.

I had to listen to the voice. My life was out of balance. My physical health was out of balance. Work had taken an exclusive priority over everything else. My so-called dream of having a school was killing me. If I hadn't attended Dr. Weiss' workshop, if I hadn't had such a spiritual experience, I believe I would have continued on the same path until my body just stopped.

At times throughout the year I would casually mention to my husband that I might no longer want to keep the school.

"What if I told you I don't want the school anymore? What if I told you it was too much for me? What if I told you I wanted to do something else?"

He would look at me and laugh, not taking me seriously.

"Don't say that. You don't mean it! This is your dream. You've worked so hard to create it."

Not having the school was a scary thought. Exploring me and other areas of my life was an even scarier thought. Yet as I sat in traffic on this lovely May morning, I remembered how I had not been scared to open the school. I remembered feeling guided, pulled by a strong force, much like the force that had pulled me to the mansion on Monterey Square. A force so strong that it didn't allow me to be afraid; in fact, I was afraid not to follow it. The force had made me feel I had to be a teacher and I had to start a school. It wasn't even a choice.

Although I always knew I was going to be a teacher when I grew up, I had been interested in other careers such as psychology, law, and even medicine. But I had felt compelled to follow this track. I had seen the vision of my school since I was a child.

I had even felt guided in my search for the building. After yet another hour looking at the boring exteriors of buildings in strip malls that were zoned for schools, I had turned to my real-estate agent.

"You don't understand that I DON'T want a standard commercial building. My school has to be in a house. An old Victorian house with a porch. It has to be a home."

I saw the house in my mind. I had pictured it for as long as I could remember.

"Do you know how hard it is to find an older Victorian home that's zoned appropriately and up to state standards for a school?" the agent had told me. "You can find an older home that's commercially zoned, but the time and money it will take to get town and state approvals, not to mention the cost to renovate and be in compliance, will drain you and may take years. You may have to settle for starting in something that's move-in ready. Why is an older Victorian home with a porch so important to you anyway?"

That was the million-dollar question. The only answer was that I felt the house. I saw the house. I had been in the house. It was what I knew. It was what felt right.

And now this dream-turned-reality didn't feel right.

As I pulled up to the school, my stomach churned. I looked out the car window at the flowers blooming from the bulbs planted by the students earlier in the year. May was such a busy month at the school, and as chief administrator I had much to do. In addition to end-of-year reports, teacher evaluations, and planning for the summer program, prom was around the corner, with graduation close behind. Add final exams, sporting events and the school cookout, and I had little time to focus on anything else. But this end of the school year was different. For the first time, my heart was no longer engaged.

I took a deep breath, painted a smile on my face and opened the front door. I longed to drive to the beach and sit along the shore with my toes in the ocean, blanketed by the warmth of the sun, inhaling the salt air as the sea mist kissed my face, while I figured out what I was supposed to learn from the recent string of events. But I knew there was no time for that. Not now. I needed to prepare for graduation. I needed to provide for my family. What I needed to do was not what I wanted to do. I wanted to find the identity of the woman who starred in my regression memories. I wanted to know why she had come to me. I was ready to go through a door and explore the past in order to leave it behind.

Perhaps what I wanted was really what I needed.

Chapter 10: Letting Go

I stood on the stage and looked out into the crowd of students, parents, friends, family, community members, and school officials who sat in the auditorium to take part in the graduation and end-of-year award ceremony. Things had certainly grown since the school's first graduation. I had opened the school with only a few students. I would like to say that things got easier as the years progressed, but they didn't. Instead of feeling accomplished and proud, I was feeling distraught and beaten. Not by the students. Seeing their accomplishments and growth kept me going. I was inspired by hearing the voice of a teenage student on the autistic spectrum who had never spoken until coming to our school, or by learning that a student who had spent most of his academic career with failing grades was now accepted to the college of his choice. What drained me of energy was the constant fight against a bureaucratic agency whose agenda was very different from mine, an agency that kept changing the rules and regulations. It was the fight to keep the school open when the state wanted all students in its public schools, meeting test score requirements without providing life jackets to students who were struggling to keep their heads above stormy waters.

The graduation ceremony was always a moving event. In addition to awards, recognitions and diplomas, a big slide show set to meaningful music depicted the school year, highlighting all the memorable experiences, relationships, and accomplishments of the year. The slide show always evoked laughter, sighs, and tears. We were not just a school; we were a family.

I was much more subdued this year. I knew what was in my heart would soon be reality. I stood at the podium, cleared my throat and began my speech.

"To thine own self be true. William Shakespeare shared these words over four hundred years ago. It was true then, and it is true now. The person who you are with most in life is yourself. Just think. If you don't like yourself, you're spending a lot of time with someone you don't like. The way to be happy is to like yourself, and the way to like yourself is to do only things that make you proud.

"To be true to yourself means to act in accordance with who you are and what you believe. As you cannot truly love anyone else unless you love yourself, you also cannot be true to anyone else until you are true to yourself. Many young people believe that when they do things to please their peers they will be popular and liked. They go against the advice of their parents, people who care about them, or their own common sense, only to find themselves in trouble and not accomplishing what they set out to do.

"Years ago, Dr. Ruth Westheimer made the statement in her commencement speech at Trinity College University that her favorite animal is the turtle. I was a bit puzzled when I first heard this. Most of the people I know would choose a dog, a cat, a horse, or something cute, furry, and warm as their favorite animal. However, in listening to her reason, I have a better understanding of why the turtle is Dr. Ruth's animal of choice. I also have a deeper appreciation for the turtle myself. Dr. Ruth's reason is that in order for the turtle to move, it has to stick its neck out. There are going to be times in your life when you're going to have to stick your neck out in order to move forward. There will be challenges, and instead of hiding in a shell, you have to go out and meet them.

"As I look at you, the students in this audience, I can't help but compare you to the turtle. The majority of you entered this school hiding in a shell you had created to protect yourself from the hurt and disappointment you had experienced in your life. You came to this school afraid to trust. Afraid to trust others, but also afraid to trust yourself. You kept your head tucked safely within your protective shell, feeling afraid and lacking the confidence to stick your neck out in order to face the challenges that seemed insurmountable."

I held eye contact with the large group of students who were attentively watching me. My eyes filled, and tears slowly trickled down my cheeks. I touched on the fact that the school provided a safe, nurturing environment that supported these students in sticking out their necks. Our school was not just about academic learning. It was about learning what is right with themselves instead of what is wrong. It was about learning to love themselves. I couldn't express my pride in these students and the privilege of watching them slowly but steadily continue to move forward, learning to be true to themselves.

"Another interesting fact about the turtle that Dr. Ruth did not mention is that if for some reason a turtle rolls onto his back, it is next to impossible for him to get back on his feet without the help of others. There will be times when you find yourself flat on your back, floundering, wondering how you will land on your feet again. There will be times when you may want to crawl back into your protective shell, hiding from the world, questioning your confidence, afraid to move forward. Don't panic. This is normal as long as you come back out of your shell the next day. If you find yourself stuck in your shell, too afraid to move forward, remember that the turtle needs help to get back on its feet, and you may need help, too, so ask. Don't struggle alone. Don't give up. Continue, like the turtle, sticking out your neck, moving steadily towards your goal, and asking for help when you need to get back on your feet. It takes courage to be true to yourself. If you believe in yourself, others will too. And if you have confidence in who you are, there is no end to what you can accomplish."

I knew this message was just as much for me as it was for the students. I also knew it would be the last speech I would give for this school.

When the ceremony ended, a plentiful buffet lunch was served in the dining hall. I cordially greeted people as I mingled and congratulated students and parents. I felt numb as I sensed that today marked more than an end to a school year.

In the dark silence that followed once the guests had left and the students had boarded their school buses to begin their summer vacation, I quietly walked outside to collect the day's mail. It was a warm June afternoon, and the humidity left me feeling sticky as I sat on a bench in front of the school, sorting through the letters, catalogs, and advertisements. I looked up from my sorting to see staff members in the parking lot, laughing and talking, eager to head home to enjoy the short reprieve before the summer program began. The glare from the sun was making my eyes water, and I wished I had remembered my sunglasses as I returned to reading the day's mail.

I didn't know what I was looking for in the mail that day, but when I came across a letter with a return address from the State Department of Education, I knew this was the one. I opened the envelope with trembling hands, my eyes blurring as I began to read the words printed on the paper bearing the department's official letterhead.

"The Commissioner's decision to hold your school to the new enrollment regulations has been upheld. Your school did not meet the new daily average enrollment criteria, therefore you do not meet the requirements to be a state-approved school. As of July 1, your school will no longer be state approved and will be strictly private, blah, blah, blah ... " The words on the page blurred and ran together.

What did this mean? This meant that I would no longer receive state money for tuition payments. This meant that parents would have to pay the tuition out of pocket, which would not be feasible for the majority of students. I would need a lawyer to fight this decision, which would be very expensive and time-consuming. This meant I had a very good reason to close the school.

"It's time to let go," the voice stated. "Your karma with the school is complete. Have faith. There are other experiences waiting for you. Let go. Move on. It's time."

I wouldn't fight the state's decision. It was time to listen to my inner voice. It was time to stick my head out from my protected shell and move forward

Chapter 11: That Person

One of the symptoms of an approaching nervous breakdown is the belief that one's work is terribly important.
— Nobel laureate Bertrand Russell (1872–1970)

It was an evening in July 2010, the summer I slowed down long enough to listen, when I was hit with a daunting question: When and how did I become *That Person*? *That Person* who seems to be losing her keys all the time. *That Person* who is always running late. *That Person* who needs to lose twenty pounds. *That Person* still struggling for financial security in her 40s. *That Person* who thought she had it all together but is breaking down in front of her children and worried she needs Xanax or help that no one can give her.

The day I saw myself as *That Person* began with plans for a fun Mommy and Daughter day with eight-year-old Jennifer. We would start by spending the afternoon at a birthday pool party for a boy in her class. Not only did I dread wearing a bathing suit, the one I owned no longer fit. I began trying on summer outfits. Even my "large on me" summer wardrobe from last year would not zipper, button, or snap over my newly found pounds. I had now crossed over into the world of *That Person* whose only choice for hiding her fat and breathing at the same time is to wear a muumuu. Great start to a Mommy and Daughter day. Like most women, I enjoy immersing myself in the refreshing water of a swimming pool. But like most women, I also feel the public eye viewing and judging when I'm not loving my body. So I did what many of us do: I stayed out of the clear, cool pool water and sat on the sidelines to sweat.

After watching my daughter swim while I chatted with other sideline Moms, next on the agenda were dinner and a drive-in movie. The closest drive-in was about an hour away in New York state. We had returned from the party at 6 p.m., so we had plenty of time to make the movie at 8:55 pm. Plenty of time unless you are *That Person* who could not organize herself to get dressed in the morning, let alone get dinner made, her daughter bathed, the dogs fed, and the car packed for the ride to the movie.

At least dinner was a success. Even *That Person* could handle the stress of preparing fried chicken cutlets, store-bought mashed potatoes, and a frozen vegetable. But I forgot that I didn't have money in my wallet to cover the movie. Going from a six-figure salary to unemployment had been, to say the least, a reality check. Okay, no cash, so I could use the debit card. No debit card. My husband had it with him. Surely I had cash somewhere. I checked another purse. No luck. Okay, kid's piggy bank. Ouch! I had already taken twelve dollars from her the other day. Only change clinked in the piggy bank. I started counting. Sixteen dollars in quarters. Whew, the movie was a go! I could stop at a change machine along the way to trade the quarters for bills.

Next up was getting the dogs ready to go with us. Two pugs; I think that says enough. I packed snacks and drinks, since obviously there was no money for the snack stand. As I rushed to prepare for our movie adventure, my daughter came to me with a pair of my summer pajamas. She was already in hers.

"Here, Mommy. I brought you these pajamas to wear to the drive-in," she said with a big smile.

They were pretty, flowered lightweight pajama pants with a spaghetti strap top. I no longer fit into them. I now wore extra-large T-shirts and sweat pants to bed. Yes, I was *That Person.* The look on my face must have reflected the way I was feeling about myself. My daughter looked at me with hurt in her eyes.

"Mommy," she said, "I thought you would be happy and surprised. I found your pajamas that almost match mine. I wanted us to be twins."

My heart sank. I now was *That Person* who didn't even acknowledge my daughter's thoughtfulness and love. Instead, I had been annoyed.

Finally, we were ready to go, 7:30 p.m., right on schedule. We headed out to the car: me, my daughter, and our two pugs, along with blankets, folding chairs, snacks, drinks, and water for the dogs. I opened my purse to get the car keys and guess what? The keys were not in my purse. They must be on the kitchen counter. I ran inside to get them. No, not on the kitchen counter. Must be in the bedroom. No, not in the bedroom. Checked my purse again. Emptied the purse. Still, no keys. I was *That Person* who forgets where she put her keys and ends up being late.

I was now officially losing it. I was crying, screaming and having conversations with myself. My daughter was consoling me. What was wrong with this picture? I had graduated to *That Person* who loses it in front of her kids. This was not good. This was not me.

I decided to empty the bag that my daughter brought with her to the pool party. There, at the bottom of the bag, were the keys! It was now 8 p.m. We could still make it by 9 p.m. and miss only the coming attractions.

We piled into the car. I had a great idea. Although I already knew where I was going, I decided to use my GPS to see if there was a faster way to the theater. Sure enough, the wonderful navigational system found a new route. I decided to trust the system, since I could no longer trust myself, and we ventured forward.

As I followed my device's directions, I realized I was going in the opposite direction. Although hesitant, I figured that the system must know a more efficient way. As we drove along roads with no names on a scenic tour through Northern New Jersey for more than an hour, I ended up lost.

"It's late," I told Jennifer. "I don't think we're going to make it to the movies. I'm so very sorry. I really made a mess of this night!"

A sweet, calm voice of reason from the back seat said to me, "It's okay, Mommy. It doesn't matter what we do. I just want to spend time with you. As long as we're together, everything is okay. I'm just having fun because I'm with you."

The tears welled in my eyes. How could I be *That Person* who forgets what is truly important? She was right. I was the one not enjoying myself because I had forgotten how to be. I had lost sight of what was important.

I concluded that I had driven this far, so, late or not, we were going forward. We reached the drive-in at 9:30 p.m. Oops, I had forgotten to stop to cash in my change. I would have to use a credit card and cross my fingers that it worked. As I pulled up to the cashier, I read the sign posted in capital letters: WE DO NOT ACCEPT CREDIT CARDS!

"I am so sorry," I said to the woman in the cashier's booth. "I have no cash and was hoping to use a credit card, but I see you don't accept them. I have enough change with me to pay for the tickets, if you just bear with me for a moment." I began to dig in my purse for the quarters.

"There's an ATM machine down the road at the local supermarket. You can get cash there," the cashier replied.

"Thank you, but I don't have a debit card with me, and I've already missed more than a half hour of the first movie." I started counting out the quarters and handed them to her one dollar at a time.

Soon another car was behind me. The cashier gave me a look. She then gave my daughter and my two pugs a similar look. Suddenly she handed me the quarters I had given her. She also handed me two tickets for the show and two dog treats for the pugs. She looked me in the eye and said, "Go and enjoy the show."

I hesitated and looked at her, bewildered.

"But I haven't paid for the tickets. Please, I do have the money. Let me finish paying you."

Having someone give and be kind to me did not feel comfortable.

The woman smiled and repeated herself, "Go enjoy the show. Use your money to treat your daughter and yourself to a snack at the snack bar."

Once again, my eyes filled with tears. This stranger gave me much more than free entry to a movie. She gave me love, hope, and good will when I so truly needed it. After closing my school and ending the years of bureaucratic bullying I had endured, here was this woman, passing along a kindness. In might have been small in her mind, but to me it was huge. Without knowing it, she had restored my faith and put things back in perspective for me. One simple act of kindness and understanding was all it took.

With tears in my eyes and a smile on my face, I thanked her and drove into the lot. I parked the car, tuned in the radio and got us all situated. Jennifer and I built a cozy haven out of blankets and pillows on top of the car roof. It was a warm, clear night, and the sky was filled with the light of stars sparkling in the distance. We gazed at the sky, snuggled, laughed and enjoyed the second movie as the dogs curled up on our laps. My daughter was wise beyond her eight years. It was late. I didn't think my daughter would last until the show ended at 1 a.m., but she surprised me and stayed awake for the entire movie.

We left the drive-in at 1:05 am. Daughter and dogs quickly fell asleep in the back seat. I turned off my navigator. I could once again trust myself to get to where I was going. I drove back the way I knew and was home in less than an hour.

In the end, it was one of the best nights of my life. Somehow, throughout the years, I had lost myself. I had allowed myself to become disconnected to the important things in life and had turned into someone I didn't recognize or like. But I am forever grateful for the loving words of my daughter and the random act of kindness from a stranger that helped to put things back in perspective. I was grateful that I recognized the blessings in a challenging day. I knew that the power to change was within.

It was July, less than a month since I had officially closed the alternative high school that I had worked so hard to create. I knew it was time to move on, to rid myself of the internal garbage that was polluting my soul. The school had needed to fall away. It would be replaced with something better, but not until I got better. I knew I needed to follow the guidance that was coming to me through visions, thoughts, and feelings. I needed to give in to what I had been fighting. I was not and would not be *That Person.*

Chapter 12: Things Get Worse Before They Get Better

A flash of enlightenment offers a preview of coming attractions, but when it fades, you will see more clearly what separates you from that state — your compulsive habits, outmoded beliefs, false associations, and other mental structures. Just when our lives are starting to get better, we may feel like things are getting worse — because for the first time we see clearly what needs to be done. — Author Dan Millman

"Who in the world am I? Ah, that's the great puzzle."
— Lewis Carroll, Alice in Wonderland

Apparently the closing of my school was the last digit to the internal combination that had kept *That Person* locked away in the corners of my soul. *That Person,* a scared child feeling alone and lost, had been protected by a life of controlled chaos, filled with doing. It was a life that had blocked out the luxury of quiet stillness and the flow of memories.

Dr. Weiss' workshop a few months earlier seemed to have triggered the crumbling of the fortress that I had painstakingly built to protect the child within. The wall had cracked, bit by bit, until the summer I closed my school, when the walls came crashing down.

The state-approved alternative high school I had created ten years earlier was my passion, built on a rich history of self-reliance and survival skills. It was a school for brilliant, sensitive souls who had been programmed to believe their authentic selves were somehow disfigured and incapable of success unless they corrected their way of functioning in the world. The system demanded completion of homework even if a student had to spend his evenings caring for his younger siblings while his alcoholic mother could not be roused from her bed. The system celebrated the student who could sit quietly at his desk, reciting information from a textbook. But the system offered little for the student who was itching to immerse himself in the creativity of a hands-on project or a field trip that allowed him to touch, absorb and imprint the material instead of reading and regurgitating it. Mandatory testing and one-size-fits-all curricula blocked these creative students and took a chainsaw to them to try to make square pegs fit into schools with round holes — with the ironic goal of no child left behind. The system no longer supported schools for square pegs and did everything in its power to squelch schools such as mine.

Dr. Weiss' workshop was perhaps divine intervention. It had allowed me to let go of the school, which had gripped my psyche for 10 years or more. It had awakened the intuitive child dormant inside me and left me standing before the crumbled fortress that lay at my feet like a jigsaw puzzle, waiting to be put back together. But how? It appeared that some pieces of my inner puzzle were missing and could only be retrieved from the depths of my soul.

I don't care for jigsaw puzzles. They are tedious and time-consuming. They require sitting quietly and fully concentrating. Dumping the box of jumbled pieces on the table can be overwhelming. Where do I begin? Do I start with the outer pieces and work my way to the inside? Do I look at the picture on the box for guidance? Do I create a plan and stick to it? What if my plan doesn't work? Do I ask others to help me complete the puzzle? What if I don't feel comfortable with the way someone else is putting my puzzle together? What if I can't find a missing piece and become frustrated? The journey starts with the first piece, followed by piece after piece, one at a time.

But unlike a jigsaw puzzle, I had no picture of what the finished product should look like.

The summer of 2010 was my first season of unemployment. Even though I was ready for change, I had underestimated how disorienting it would be. The morning after the drive-in movie episode with *That Person,* I struggled to open my eyes and adjust to the sunlight shining through my window, ending a dark and fretful sleep. I fumbled for my eyeglasses on the table next to my bed and looked at the alarm clock: Seven a.m. My husband was lying next to me snoring. The house was quiet, and I fought the urge to throw the covers over my head and hide all day under the blankets. Facing the day had been difficult lately. For the first time in my adult life I had no job to report to in the morning. I had no one counting on me to show up and resolve conflicts, answer questions, teach, guide. It left me with an uneasy feeling of no longer knowing who I was. My purpose in life escaped me. I had lived so many years defining myself by what I do. I am a teacher. I am a supervisor. I am a principal. I am an executive director. I am a business owner. I am lost.

I forced myself to sit up and placed my feet on the floor. I sat on the edge of the bed, staring into space, waiting for motivation, a reason to rise and start my day. The dogs must have sensed my stirring, for soon my motivation for getting up was to quiet their barking from the floor below. I descended the stairs and opened the front door to let the dogs out. I walked into the kitchen eager to make the coffee. The smell of the fresh brew awakened my senses, and pouring the first cup of the day infused me with a pleasing calm. I savored the first sip as the coffee's warmth soothed me from the inside out. After feeding the dogs, I picked up my journal, pen, and coffee and went outside to the front porch. I sat in the rocking chair, watching the summer's dew sparkle on the grass in the morning sun and slowly sipped my coffee, enjoying this moment of being alone. As I sat in solitude with the July sun in my face, I realized that much of my life had taken place without me questioning or putting much thought into why things happened the way they did. Perhaps on some level I purposely kept myself too busy, not allowing myself the time to question my life decisions. When I kept every minute of my day filled with commitments and taking care of others, it made it easier to push aside any thoughts or questions about myself and the direction my life was taking.

I opened my journal, picked up my pen and began to write. I just allowed my hand to write whatever my mind was saying without filtering or organizing the flow of the words. Questions began racing in my mind, and my hand and pen could barely keep up with the pace. How did I get to this point in my life? Why didn't my father love me? Why does the relationship with my mother continue to be so difficult? Who am I without a title? What am I supposed to learn? How will I leave my mark on this world? How will I reinvent myself? Where do I go from here? Will I get it right this time? How will I make it through the day? I want a better life, but how do I go about getting one?

I put my pen down and read the words I had written. As I gently rocked in my chair and sipped my coffee, my eyes locked in on one question: Why didn't my father love me? It became obvious to me that the void created by having an absent father might still be haunting me. Although I spent years convincing myself that our lack of relationship was his loss, not mine, it occurred to me at this moment that it was my loss, too, a loss that I apparently had yet to reconcile. I always felt that I knew the relationship I was intended to have with my father, but reality didn't fit with the picture imprinted in my heart. I allowed my mind to return to a place and time that I hadn't dared to go for many years. I knew that my healing process needed to begin with confronting and forgiving hurts of the past. I soon found myself back in my childhood home, reliving experiences as if they had happened yesterday.

My mother kissed me goodbye before closing the door behind her. I watched out the dining room window as she backed the car out of the driveway and left for work. It was Saturday morning, and my mother was off to her part-time job at a gift shop located a few towns away. I felt a twinge of sadness while I watched the car and my mother move out of sight. I took a deep breath and looked around the room. The house felt empty. Although my father was home to care for me, I couldn't help but feel alone. I didn't mind being alone. In fact, I often enjoyed it. I had spent my eight years of life as an only child and had learned how to entertain myself without the companionship of siblings. But being alone and feeling alone are two different things.

I walked to the stairs of our Cape Cod house and began the climb to my bedroom. There were only two rooms on the second floor of our house — mine and the den. The den was used as a sewing room by my mother and as an office by my father. Many nights I would be either lulled to sleep or awakened by the repetitive hum of my mother's sewing machine or the sound of typewriter keys pounding the paper my father was writing for his master's degree.

I went into my bedroom, sat on my bed, hugged my Polly Dolly, and listened to the sounds of the outdoors coming through my open window. It was a sunny, warm morning, and I could hear our neighbor's lawn mower and smell the sweet aroma of freshly cut grass. Listening to the screaming sounds of children running through the neighborhood, dogs barking, and people talking brought me a sense of comfort. It was reassuring to know that while the air was still and lifeless in my house, life flourished outside these walls.

I grabbed my notebook and pencil from my desk. I slipped out of my room and quietly began to descend the stairs. I stopped halfway and sat on the step right before the start of the banister railing. This allowed me to remain hidden by the wall while I peered out over the railing to spy on my father. My father was a mystery to me. His dark hair looked shiny, black, and wet from the oil that slicked it to the side of his head. He didn't talk much and showed little, if any, interest in me. I peeked over the railing to see him sitting on the couch in the living room with his socked feet resting on the coffee table. Sitting next to him was an open jar of peanut butter with a spoon in it and a section of the newspaper. He was entranced by sports on the television and seemed oblivious to my presence in the house. I decided to spend part of the day spying on him, as if he were an endangered species in a zoo. I recorded my observations in my notebook. Today, I was on a secret mission to solve the mystery of "who is my father?"

Some things I knew about my father. I knew he kept magazines of naked women in his briefcase and that they upset my mother. I knew he had a younger sister who looked like Marilyn Monroe. I knew that when he was younger he had been in a bad car accident that left him with a limp and a large scar on his arm. I knew he was a scientist and worked with animals.

I loved going with my mother to visit my father at his job. His laboratory had so many cute animals in cages, and I especially enjoyed visiting the monkeys. I kept begging my father to bring me home one of the adorable monkeys for a pet. One day he did bring home a dog. She was supposed to be a family pet, but she spent most of her time outside, chained to a doghouse and rarely allowed in our home. I worried about the dog outside all day and all night, especially in the cold winter. My mother put shag carpeting in the doghouse to make it warmer. That only helped a little to make me feel better. I spent time with the dog by crawling into the doghouse with her.

For some reason, the dog was afraid of my father and would quiver and hide when he was near. It was obvious that my father enjoyed this because he would deliberately tease the dog and laugh as the dog shook uncontrollably. I came home from school one day to find the dog gone. My mom sat me down to tell me that she had taken the dog to the vet and had her put to sleep. As she fought back the tears, my mother explained that the dog would be better off because my father didn't like her and it was not fair to keep an animal chained outside. Years later I would learn that neighbors had reported my parents to the Humane Society about leaving the dog out in the cold.

My mother insisted I greet my father at the door when he came home from work, even though he obviously didn't like it. I would be playing or watching cartoons when my mother gave me the ten-minute warning. "Your father will be home soon," she would announce. "Please be sure to clean up and be ready to greet him." The next announcement from my mother came when she saw my father's car pulling in the driveway.

"Your father's home!" That was my cue to come greet him at the back door. The welcome home greeting consisted of a hug and a kiss, which went unreturned by my father.

I knew my mother wanted me to be happy that my father was home. I wanted to feel happy, but the truth is that I didn't. I felt only confusion as my father brushed off my affection and rolled his eyes with annoyance each evening as I greeted him at the door.

There was something else I knew about my father. Something that shocked me. I had learned that my father could cry. I saw him do this when I was in kindergarten. It was an image and a night I will never forget. It was a stormy evening, and my father was away in Atlantic City on a business trip. I was brushing my teeth and getting ready for bed when the phone rang. My mother answered the phone in the kitchen, and I could tell by the sound of her voice that something was wrong. I could also hear my aunt's voice on the other end of the phone. She was screaming. She was crying.

"I'm not sure calling your brother with this news is the best thing to do right now," I heard my mother say to her sister-in-law. "The weather's bad, and I'm afraid for him driving home in this storm, especially when he'll be so upset. Maybe we should wait until morning, and someone can drive him home. There's nothing he could do by coming home tonight, and it's dangerous for him to be driving." I heard more sobbing and screaming coming from my aunt. "Yes, alright, I'll call him," my mother said with a sigh.

I looked into my mother's eyes. I could feel her fear, her anxiety.

"What's happened?" I asked. "Why do you have to call Daddy? Is he coming home?" My mother took my hands and with tears in her eyes told me that Grandpa, Daddy's father, had suffered a heart attack and died. I wasn't sure I understood, yet before I could respond, my mother was leading me upstairs to my room.

"It's time for you to go to bed. This is not going to be easy, and your father will need my attention," my mother explained as she tucked my blankets around me.

We said prayers and asked God to please help my father get home safely in the storm.

Before I knew it, my mother turned off my bedroom lights and quietly left my room, leaving me alone to deal with this news. I quickly got up, collected all my stuffed animals and tucked them into bed with me. I stayed in my bed, comforting my stuffed animals, listening to my mother on the phone, and waiting for my father's return.

I don't know how long it was before I heard the back door open. I knew it was late. I jumped out of bed and ran down the stairs to greet him, this time without being told. I was not prepared for what I saw. There my father stood, in the doorway of the kitchen, his black overcoat wet with rain and his face also wet, but not from the rain. He was crying. In fact, he was sobbing. He was shaking. For the first time, I remember hugging my father because I wanted to. There, the three of us stood in the kitchen while my mother and I hugged my distraught father. This time, my father hugged me back. My parents didn't hug, kiss, hold hands or show affection towards one another.

This was something new to me, and I liked it. We all seemed to like it, to need it. I wanted this moment to last.

It didn't last. Soon I was being sent back to my room to be alone with the mystery of what was transpiring this evening. I normally didn't feel afraid or uncomfortable alone in my room. This night was different.

As I lay in bed trying to shut out the sounds of the rain and thunder so I could fall asleep, overwhelming waves of cold air kept hitting me, sending goose bumps running up and down my body. Wrapping myself in my sheets and blankets was not enough to warm the chill that was plaguing me this night.

I don't know how long I stayed in bed watching shadows float across my bedroom walls, pulling the covers over my head, waiting for the lightning to brighten my room while anticipating the rumble of the thunder. Suddenly it hit me. I was scared. Not from the darkness that enveloped my room, not from the storm rattling my windows, not from my grandfather's death. I was scared to be alone with my thoughts and feelings. I wanted to be with my parents.

I threw off the covers, jumped out of bed, and ran downstairs to crawl in bed with my parents. I wanted more hugs. I wanted to feel the warmth of human touch and rid myself of the waves of cold that had invaded my body.

I stood by my parents' bedroom door and held my breath before turning the knob. I slowly opened the door and entered my parents' dark room to the sound of sobbing. As my eyes adjusted to the darkness, I could see my father sitting on the edge of the bed, holding his head in his hands. He was still crying as my mother sat next to him rubbing his back. I envisioned my mother taking me in her arms, comforting me, allowing me to be part of this grieving, including me in the giving and sharing of love and support. I stood beside my parents' bed, waiting for them to embrace me. Instead, my parents looked at me as though I had done something wrong.

Between sobs, my father turned to my mother and said, "Get her out of here!"

I stood there in the dark bedroom not believing what I heard. Weren't we all just hugging each other in the kitchen? I couldn't have been the only one who wanted more of that. Certainly my mother would understand. She would embrace and welcome my presence. My mother did reach for me, but only to firmly take me by the hand. She was angry that I had disobeyed her by getting out of bed. She was annoyed that I had disturbed my parents when they needed privacy. She led me out of her room and sternly told me to get back into bed and stay there.

As I climbed the stairs to my room, I felt a breeze softly brush beside me and gently guide me to my destination. From the corner of my eye, I saw my grandfather standing by the window in my room, wearing a tweed jacket. He smiled and winked at me, and I felt strongly that he was okay. In the second it took me to blink my eyes, my grandfather was gone. I jumped in bed and pulled the covers to my chin. I then felt the breeze kiss my cheek as I drifted off to sleep.

The next day in school I had Show and Tell. I walked to the front of the classroom, faced my fellow students and announced to my kindergarten classmates that my Grandpa died. Then I just stood there. Waiting. I didn't know what I was waiting for. Soon I felt the warmth of my teacher's arms wrapped around me as she pulled me close and held me tightly. I silently cried into her soft shoulder while the images of the previous night, still fresh in my memory, raced before me. There, in the arms of my teacher, I received the comfort I had longed for.

My grandfather's death was the first time I saw my father cry, and I hadn't seen him cry again since that night. As I sat on the stairs observing my father, I noticed how he seemed to be happiest when he was alone. He did things he would never do if my mother were home, like putting his feet on the coffee table, eating peanut butter from a jar, spending the day watching television, and ignoring me. He interacted more with the TV by yelling at bad plays, cheering for good ones, and laughing out loud if he saw something funny.

I watched as my father left the comfort of the couch. I scooted down the stairs and hid under the table in the dining room so I could have a clear vision of my father in the kitchen. He belched, placed the peanut butter back in the cabinet and picked up the receiver of the phone hanging on the kitchen wall.

I watched and listened as my father slowly dialed the numbers on the phone. I knew he was calling his mother. It was something he seemed to do only when my mother was at work. It caused many heated arguments between my parents. My mother found this behavior sneaky. Why couldn't he talk to his mother while my mother was home? What was he hiding? I quickly added this phone call in my notepad. I loved my grandmother dearly and would love to talk to her, but my father never asked me if I wanted to, and I knew not to ask.

One Saturday, after a phone call to my grandma, my father, in a stern tone, told me to get in the car. We both sat in silence as I watched out the car window and determined from the familiar scenery that we were headed to my grandmother's house.

I loved visiting my grandmother. She was fun, silly, and made me laugh. I loved her house and loved dressing up in her clothes, wearing her jewelry, and sashaying in her mink stole while clopping around in her high-heeled shoes. After dressing and jeweling, my grandmother would let me put on her makeup and didn't worry that I would make a big mess. Beautiful blue eye shadow, thick black eyeliner, ruby red lips, and rose-blushed cheeks. Gorgeous! The finishing touches included a hand-held fan from my aunt's fan collection, a stylish hat, long black evening gloves, and a cigarette. My grandmother placed cigarettes in beautiful vintage Victorian glass shoes, which she arranged on coffee tables and dry sinks throughout her home, making for easy access for my dress-up needs.

When my hair, make-up, and dress up were complete, I loved to walk around my grandma's neighborhood. One time, my grandmother took my hand and walked in the neighborhood with me. She brought me door to door to introduce me to her neighbors as a friend of hers visiting from out of town. It was so funny. I think the neighbors actually believed my grandma! One neighbor even invited us in for tea and cookies! What a great day!

The Saturday that my father put me in the car without telling me where we were going was different from other trips we had taken to my grandmother's. The air in the stale car was thicker than usual. No sporting events wailed from the car radio, breaking the uncomfortable silence. An anger that flashed in my father's eyes told me not to speak. I sat in the back seat of the car, listening to my father deeply inhale the smoke from his Winston cigarette. I watched as the glow from the burning ember slid down the white paper until it reached the cigarette's filter. I watched as he ground the stub of the cigarette into the ashtray of the car, putting to death what was left of the cigarette, only to immediately light another, and repeat the process. A process I couldn't understand. A process that made me feel sick.

I turned my head to look out the window and could feel the excitement grow inside me as we approached my grandmother's house. Seeing her would make things better.

My father pulled the car into the gravel driveway, and I put my hand on the door handle, eager to get out of the car and see my grandma. My father turned to me and said, "No! You need to wait in the car."

"Why?" I said. "I want to see Grandma!"

"Grandma is sick today, and I need to check on her. You stay in the car and don't come in the house!" he said.

I rolled down the window and hung my head out the car like a dog sniffing the air. I could hear my aunt and father raising their voices inside the house. I could hear glass bottles clanking, water running in the kitchen sink, and my aunt sobbing. The fall season had begun to turn the leaves lovely shades of gold, but the sun was warm, and I was getting hot sitting in the car. Why couldn't I go in the house and see my grandma? I opened the car door and stepped into my grandmother's driveway. I walked slowly, hoping no one would hear the rocks from the driveway crunch beneath my feet. I reached the side screen door and took my time opening it to keep it silent. I stood inside the small vestibule and peered into the kitchen. My beautiful aunt sat at the table in her robe, barely recognizable, rollers falling from her hair, and her tear-streaked face black with mascara stains.

"I was not home last night," I heard her explain to my father between her sobs. "When I came home, Mom was already in bed. I didn't realize she had the alcohol. She must have had it delivered. I'm sorry. It's not my fault."

My father stood at the kitchen sink, pouring clear liquid from a clear glass bottle down the drain. Several other empty glass bottles lined the counter next to the sink. After draining the bottles and running the faucet to wash the sink clean, he turned and grabbed the telephone book. He was looking through the Yellow Pages and writing on a pad while my aunt sat crying. My father dialed and told the person on the other end never to deliver alcohol to my grandma's address. After he made a few calls, he turned back around, gathered the glass bottles, and headed in my direction. I escaped from the house in time but couldn't move fast enough to make it back in the car. My father opened the screen door to find me standing in the driveway.

"What are you doing?" he growled at me. "You were to stay in the car!"

"I want to see Grandma!" I said. "I want to say hi and make sure she's alright!"

"Your grandmother is in bed and can't be disturbed," he said. "Now get back into the car! We're leaving after I throw away these bottles."

I obediently went to the car and crawled into the back seat. My father slipped behind the steering wheel, started the engine and drove home without saying a word.

I took a deep breath and broke the silence. "Daddy, is Grandma going to be okay?"

"She'll be fine," he assured me. "She's just sick."

It was a sickness that I wouldn't understand until I was much older.

As I continued to sit under the dining room table spying on my father while he spoke on the phone to my grandma, I could tell that this phone call would be okay. There would be no screaming, crying, or having to leave. In fact, my father was telling my grandma jokes that I didn't understand but that I knew were not appropriate for me to repeat. My father began speaking to his mother in a silly baby voice that he sometimes used with her. He seemed to be speaking gibberish, and I couldn't understand him. The conversation ended, and my father hung up the phone, yawned, grabbed some potato chips and went back to the living room to watch more television.

I had seen enough for now. I crawled out from under the dining room table, climbed the stairs, and put my notebook back in my room. I grabbed a book and a blanket and ran down the stairs and out the back door. I spread the blanket underneath the pine tree in the back yard, sprawled out, and inhaled the sweet scent of pine. The branches of the soft pine enveloped me in safety, reassuring me that I was not alone. Being around my father, I felt a sense of loneliness. Here under the pine tree I was surrounded by nature and a spiritual calm. A calm that would get me through the darkest hours.

"Mommy, mommy." I was suddenly brought back to the present as my daughter stood on the porch in her bare feet and pajamas, gently calling my name. Her curly hair was a tousled mess, and it was obvious that she had just rolled out of bed. Seeing her brought a smile to my face. I opened my arms, and she jumped on my lap. Together we sat on the porch, not saying a word, as we slowly rocked in the chair, watching the morning sun and the world awaken. She nuzzled her head on my chest, and I kissed her forehead. My reason to start my day was clear, and at least one piece fit securely into the puzzle of my life.

Chapter 13: Early Calling, Early Trauma

Life can only be understood backwards, but it must be lived forwards. — Søren Kierkegaard (1813–1855)

It was early evening, and the summer sun of August was setting. Nearly two months had passed since my school closed, and it felt odd to be at home, enjoying the warm night air instead of working at school to prepare for the new academic year. I stood on the deck of my house watching my daughter and the neighbor children running in the back yard, holding tightly to their jars, awaiting the first flash of light from the fireflies. I was in awe as I witnessed the joy of children who were nowhere else but in the present moment, soaking up the pleasure of glimpsing the mystery and beauty of nature. They were not worried about tomorrow or yesterday. They just wanted to hold the mystery in their hands.

My daughter jumped and reached towards the sky, cupping her fingers, attempting to capture the small, flickering light that escaped her. She smiled and turned as the six-year-old neighbor boy called out, "Look! Over here! I caught one!" My daughter squealed with delight as she ran over to look at the mysterious bug in the jar that her friend was holding. Together, they studied the magical light emitted from their find and determined that the glow was a cross between neon yellow and green. After coming to this conclusion, they released the creature from the jar and set it free to light the evening sky. They watched as the bug took flight. Soon they were off again, chasing the flicker of the lights encircling the back yard. It was that simple. It was that beautiful.

I realized that children seem to be naturally guided by spirit. They instinctively take the time to connect with nature, life, and self. As I stood on the deck listening to the laughter of the children, I realized I had allowed myself to lose touch with my inner child. I leaned against the deck railing and stared out into the evening sky, observing the children engaged in play. A warm breeze swept across my body as I watched the children who had moved to my daughter's playhouse, taking on the various roles of a family.

I continued watching and listening to the children and soon found myself back in my childhood home, playing the part that would become my adult identity.

I stood in front of the slate blackboard in the classroom I had created in the basement of our house. I spent many hours teaching my dolls and stuffed animals how to read books, write letters, and solve simple math problems. I wore a long dress and my hair was pulled back in a bun. I was a teacher from a bygone era. My classroom had old wooden Victorian desks, inkwells, and a pretend fireplace to provide warmth in the colder months. I was a structured but loving teacher, confident in my ability to instill pride, discipline, and manners in my students. I was self-assured and in control of my class.

"One apple plus one apple equals how many apples?" I asked the class. "Who would like to come to the board and solve the problem?" Polly Dolly quickly raised her hand. "Thank you, Polly, but you just answered the last question. Let's give someone else a chance now." I looked across the sea of students sitting before me. "Teddy, why don't you come up here and give it a try?" Teddy was having difficulty with numbers and needed some extra guidance.

Hesitantly, Teddy approached and stood in front of the blackboard. I repeated the problem to him.

"One apple plus one more apple equals how many apples?"

Teddy just stood there staring blankly at the board, trembling. I sprinted to my desk and took two apples that students had given me. I handed one apple to Teddy and asked, "How many apples do you have?"

He looked at the apple in his hand and answered, "One."

"That's right!" I replied. "I'm going to give you one more apple."

Teddy took the apple in his other hand. "Now, Teddy, how many apples do you have?"

He stared at one hand, then the other and slowly started to count. "One. Two. I have two apples!"

"Very good, Teddy. That is correct. So, Teddy, one apple plus one more apple equals how many apples?"

Teddy thought for a minute while the rest of the class sighed in disgust.

"Class, you need to be quiet and patient while Teddy thinks, just like he is patient when someone is learning."

Suddenly, a huge smile spread across Teddy's face. "Two apples! One apple plus one apple equals two apples!" he squealed. Teddy handed me the apples, took the chalk in his hand and proudly wrote the number two on the chalkboard. The class cheered and praised him for a job well done. What a great ending to the school day.

I assigned homework, supervised the classroom cleanup, had the students form a line, and dismissed in an orderly fashion. I then sat at my desk, corrected the classwork, and entered the grades in the grade book. I was sure to have my plans for the next day ready before I locked up my classroom and began my journey home.

On the other side of the basement, my parents had a playhouse built for me. The house was secured into the ceiling and walls of the basement and was a permanent structure. It was a fairly large house that was made to resemble our Cape Cod home. After a long day teaching, I would return home to my playhouse to rest and prepare for another day of teaching.

I took out my pots and pans and began cooking myself dinner on my play stove with light-up burners. I was just sitting down to enjoy my meal of plastic chicken and peas when my mother called down to me from atop the basement stairs. "Wash up for dinner. Your father will be home soon."

I left my playhouse and went around the basement pulling the long strings attached to the light bulbs that hung from the ceiling. Once all the lights were turned off, I ran upstairs and into the bathroom to wash my hands. As the cool water from the bathroom sink fell between my fingers, I deeply inhaled the aroma of the fried chicken that my mother had spent the afternoon preparing. My two favorite meals for dinner were fried chicken and BBQ spareribs with mashed potatoes and gravy. I couldn't wait to eat tonight. I wasn't always hungry for dinner and didn't usually like to take the time out of my creative play to settle down and eat. However, I had a busy day teaching my students, and fried chicken was one of my favorites, so tonight I was actually looking forward to dinner.

I dried my hands and walked back to the kitchen.

"Perfect timing," my mother said as she used the tongs to take the chicken out of the sizzling frying pan and place it on the platter lined with paper towels. "Please finish setting the table and don't forget the salad dressing from the refrigerator."

Without a word, I opened the utensil drawer and took out three forks, three knives, and three spoons. I carefully set the fork to the left of the plate while placing the knife and then spoon to the right. I folded the napkins to look like triangles and placed them alongside the fork. I went to the refrigerator and took out bottles of salad dressing, being sure to remember the only dressing I would eat, Kraft French, and placed the bottles on the table.

My mother was busy whipping the mashed potatoes, careful to add just the right amount of butter, milk, and salt. As we were working together in the kitchen, we both saw headlights of my father's car shine through the window. I could hear the car door slam and held my breath as I waited to see my father's dark silhouette enter the back door of the kitchen. Soon the door opened and there stood my father. He did not enter the room with his arms opened wide and ask, "How are my girls?" He did not sniff the air and comment on the delicious aroma of home cooking that filled the kitchen and delighted the senses. He was just there.

I knew what I had to do and walked over to him, gave him a hug and said, "Hi, Daddy. How was your day?" He did what he usually did and put down his briefcase, took off his coat, and went to his bedroom to take off his tie and cuff links.

My mother and I finished bringing the food to the table. My father joined us, and we all sat down to eat. The family dinnertime started out to be enjoyable. I had told a few jokes that made my parents laugh, and my father shared a story about a woman who worked with him. I lost interest in the conversation and entertained myself by pretending that the gravy in the center of my mashed potatoes was actually a lake and the potatoes surrounding it were mountains. My fork would cliff dive from the potato-mountains and land in the gravy lake. At some point while I was lost in my imagination and playing with my food, the conversation between my mother and father had taken a nasty turn.

I snapped out of my fork having to rescue my spoon from the muddy lake water to hear the tone of my mother's voice become angry and shrill as she accused my father of comparing her cooking to that of his mother's. I felt my body tense as my eyes gazed at the food remaining on my plate. I pretended I was invisible, which is how I felt the majority of time in the presence of my parent's arguing. I knew this scene all too well. I held my breath and grabbed tightly to the seat of my chair in preparation for what was to come.

I watched from the corner of my eye as my mother picked up my father's dinner plate and threw it to the ground. I closed my eyes and flinched as pieces of the dinner plate exploded and flew in the air. For a quick instance my mother remembered I was still sitting there at the table and through gritted teeth, she sternly ordered me to go to my room. I got up from my chair, left the kitchen and climbed the stairs to my room. I closed my bedroom door, grabbed my Raggedy Ann, and sprawled out on my bed, staring at the ceiling. I listened as my parents screamed, yelled, and became physical with each other. I didn't cry when this happened anymore. I had become numb to it. The fighting between my parents happened often and in the presence of others. In the presence of my friends.

At times, when this had happened in the past, I would run from the house and cross the street to the home of Mr. Schaffer, a police officer. I would stand on his porch, banging on his door crying for him to please help stop my parents from fighting before someone got hurt. There were times when my mother would scream for me to get Mr. Schaffer because she claimed my father was hurting her. Mr. Schaffer did come to break up the fight once or twice, but after a while, he stopped answering his door.

My parents' fight had moved from the kitchen to their bedroom where I could still hear bits and pieces of the arguing through the vent in my room. I got up from my bed and sat at my vanity table. I picked up my brush and began brushing my hair. "One, two, three." As I began counting each stroke of the brush, I immediately felt a sense of gratitude that my hair was almost as long as it was prior to my traumatizing haircut. My long, dark, curled hair was very important to me, and I never wanted to lose it again.

My mother was not a fan of my long hair and wanted it short. She would get angry having to wash, dry, detangle, curl, and style it. She felt long hair was vain and impractical. "Short hair is much easier to manage," she would say. Although I was only six years old, I knew my need for long hair ran deeper than vanity. It was part of my identity. In my heart I felt it was wrong for me to have short hair. It went against my beliefs. It went against something I knew I had been previously taught.

As I stared in the mirror brushing my hair, the memory of my first haircut came rushing back to me. It was spring, and I was enjoying my last year of nursery school. I was officially five years old and would begin real school in the fall.

"Summer is approaching, and short hair will be cool and easy to manage in the hot weather," my mother had said.

I took another bite of my sandwich, swallowed and looked at my mother.

"My hair won't make me hot," I answered calmly. "I can wear it in pony or pigtails. I don't want short hair. I wouldn't be happy with my hair cut short."

I could tell by the way my mother sighed and turned away that she was disgusted. I continued eating my lunch, knowing somehow that the conversation was not over.

"So many of your friends have those cute pixie style haircuts. Wouldn't you like one, too?"

"No." I said. "I like long hair."

"Okay," my mother said. "How about just getting your hair trimmed?"

"What is that?" I asked.

"A trim is when just a small amount of hair is cut from your length to help keep your hair even and healthy," she said.

"Will my hair still be long?" I asked.

"Of course it will!" my mother promised.

I gave in and agreed to get my hair trimmed. During the car ride to the hair salon, I kept asking my mother, "Are you sure my hair will still be long?"

She kept reassuring me, "Yes, it will still be long."

I sat in the salon chair as the stylist took the scissors in her hand and began to cut. My eyes filled with tears as I soon realized that I was getting my hair cut short. I was getting a pixie cut. I cried as I saw my beautiful long locks lying on the floor.

"Why isn't my hair still long?" I asked the stylist after she finished cutting. "I was supposed to have a trim."

"Oh, no, honey. Your mommy asked for your hair to be cut short," the stylist said. "Don't you like it?"

The tears rolling down my cheeks answered her question. She bent down, picked up pieces of my long hair from the floor, and wrapped the hair in tissue paper for me to take home. I was hoping there would be some way for me to glue these pieces of hair back onto my head.

After that haircut, I closed myself in my room and refused to be seen. I was embarrassed to go school or play with my friends. I spent hours pulling on my hair in hopes it would grow faster. It wasn't a pretty haircut, and I felt I looked like a boy. I was so very sad. Didn't anyone understand that a girl was not supposed to cut her hair? I knew this. I also now knew something about my mother. It was not only my hair that I would no longer trust with her.

I was startled out of my daze as my mother entered my room. I was embarrassed to have her see me sitting and looking at myself in the mirror, but she didn't seem to notice.

"Time to get ready for bed," my mother instructed.

I put on my pajamas and went downstairs to brush my teeth. My father was sitting in the living room watching television. I went in and said good night to him. My mother walked with me back to my bedroom. We read and said prayers, and she tucked me into bed. Nothing was mentioned about the fight, and nothing ever would be. Life would resume as if nothing had happened.

The happy squeals from the children and the coolness of the evening air brought me back to the present. The clear, black summer sky was brilliant with sparkling, vivid stars whose dazzling glow created a halo in the darkness. The children were gazing at the night sky, pointing to what they thought might be constellations, planets, planes, and fairies. I heard my daughter reciting, "Star light, star bright, the first star I see tonight, I wish I may, I wish I might, have this wish I wish tonight."

I watched as she closed her eyes, crinkled her forehead, and silently made her wish.

It was getting late. I called for my daughter to come inside. I said goodbye to the neighbor children and watched as they walked home to the house next door.

As I tucked Jennifer into bed and turned off her bedroom light, she said, "I love my life, mommy. Thank you for saving me."

I hugged her tightly, kissed her and said, "I love you so very much. Thank you for being in my life."

I sometimes forgot that she was adopted. I felt as though Jennifer had been with me forever and not just a few years. My son, Michael, was in high school when she entered our lives. I thought my days of parenting were coming to an end. We didn't plan to adopt, but when the opportunity presented itself for us to provide her with foster care and later adoption, we couldn't refuse.

After saying goodnight to Jennifer, I walked into my bedroom, kicked off my flip-flops, and fell onto my bed. I lay on my back and stared at the ceiling, reflecting on the children this evening who seemed to be so in touch with their intuition and the wonders of nature. When did I stop chasing fireflies? When did I stop wishing on stars? When had I taken the time to really look at the stars? Why?

As a child, I needed to take walks in the woods. I needed to look at the stars. I needed to daydream. It came as naturally as breathing. As a child, I didn't question my intuition. I relied on it. My sensitivity and awareness took away the self-doubt that would creep into my mind. I had allowed myself to lose touch with my intuition, with my spirituality, with me. For years, I had been suppressing and ignoring the voice inside me that had been telling me to stop, to slow down, to live life.

I had been consumed with running my business, taking care of the students, the staff, the building, the parents. I had lost sight of who really needed my care. I was consumed with pleasing outside authorities who were dictating their truths to me and to my business. How many times had I hidden my annoyance at having to stop working to read bedtime stories, go to my children's school functions, or attend their sporting events? I had, after all, forgotten my daughter's concert on that important night. Was I ever as resentful of my children as my father seemed to be with me? How many times had I returned friends' calls out of obligation, not because I wanted to connect and talk? How many times had I skipped parties or made excuses not to do things alone with my husband because I had too much work to do? How many times had I pretended to be listening or enjoying something only to be preoccupied with working on my internal to-do list, just as I had disappeared into my childhood teaching duties or tuned out my parents' arguments to seek solace from my stuffed animals? How long had I been on autopilot? How much living had I missed?

It was time I reconnected with the child I had hidden. I decided it was time to work with her instead of against her. We would work on the jigsaw puzzle together.

Chapter 14: The Mystery of My Father

You have to leave the city of your comfort and go into the wilderness of your intuition. You can't get there by bus, only by hard work and risk and by not quite knowing what you're doing, but what you'll discover will be wonderful. What you'll discover will be yourself. — Alan Alda

It seems as though no matter how hot and humid August gets, once September hits, there is a different feel in the air. It is the feeling of fall being right around the corner. It is the feeling of a fresh start. The feeling of a new school year, new clothes, new pencils, new notebooks, new beginnings. This was the first September since I was a child that I would not be returning to school.

I had officially made it through my first summer of unemployment. I had my children home with me. I had purpose. It felt more acceptable to be unemployed for a summer, filling my days with going to the beach, reading novels, and relaxing on the porch. Fall meant back to work, back to routine, back to following a schedule. I now faced the most difficult risk of my life — the risk of letting go without a plan. I had to move from my city of comfort with extreme care, knowing that change must begin from the inside out, putting complete trust in my intuition as I walked into the wilderness of the unknown.

Okay. What was I to do now? Jennifer was off to school. Michael was back in college. I had nowhere to go. I had no career commitment. This was unfamiliar terrain, and I was traveling without a compass. I always had dreamed of being a "stay-at-home mom," standing at the bus stop in the morning with the other stay-at-home moms, with my travel mug of coffee in one hand, my well-behaved Golden Retriever leashed in the other, wearing a stylish warm-up suit with matching running shoes, prepared to take my morning walk once the children were safely on the bus.

This morning did not play out quite like my dream. I did take a jog this morning, but it was only because Jennifer and I were running to catch the bus. Unfortunately, I do not own cute workout clothes with matching sneakers and was wearing pajama pants, an oversized T-shirt, and flip-flops. I also do not own a Golden Retriever, and my undisciplined Pugs were getting their exercise by chasing each other around the kitchen island.

Deep breath. Now what? I stood in the kitchen leaning against the counter and scanned the main level of my 4,000-square-foot home. We had been able to purchase the home two years earlier because the school was doing well and the government hadn't cut funding. I thought I was fulfilling my life purpose, my dream.

But that was before I had met Dr. Brian Weiss and had leaped into the void of a new search for meaning. Now I found myself questioning my life purpose, questioning what I was lacking on the inside that I had tried to fill by buying such a large home.

I had wanted to open a school so badly that I let nothing stop me. I had wanted to buy this home so badly that I let nothing stop me. So why was I feeling a bit resentful towards both the school and my house? Be careful what you wish for. Did this statement apply to my situation? I had allowed the school to own my life and had let my strong work ethic turn me a full-blown workaholic, and I might have stayed there until it killed me.

But that was the past. No mistakes, only lessons. Regroup. Let's look at this as a sabbatical. A time to learn and grow. An opportunity for me to explore the visions of my regressions and see if I can find an explanation, a truth. The truth had always enticed me. As a child, it was chronically elusive in the web of lies and deceit spun in my family. As an adult, I often found that I lied to myself, only to bear the painful consequences eventually.

To thine own self be true was much easier said than done. It was also very difficult to be true to an unknown. I needed to get to know myself. I felt as if I had known myself better as a child. It was the people around me I had struggled to know. As a child I had tried so hard to understand my father, yet he passed away before I ever really knew him, perhaps before anyone truly knew him, including himself.

I felt that understanding my relationship to my father was a key to understanding myself. He had created even more mystery in his death in 2001. Yet he also had shown me that we were connected not just by blood but by spirit, and I had learned that I could love him even if I wasn't sure I liked him.

It was December 5, 2001. My husband awoke late that night to find me no longer in bed. He followed the soft glow of light that led him to our home office. He found me sitting at the computer, my fingers quickly typing and my eyes staring at the screen, searching for answers. Mark gently placed his hand on my shoulder and asked, "What are you doing? You need to be asleep."

I turned to him with a tear-streaked face and said, "I have to do it now. I don't have much time left." Mark looked at me lovingly, yet quizzically.

"Time left for what?" he asked.

"To find my father," I said. "He'll be leaving this life soon. If I don't contact him now, I soon won't have the chance."

"We'll find him," Mark whispered.

But I already knew there was not enough time. My father had deliberately changed his phone number to an unpublished one so no family members could reach him, not even his mother or his sister. It had been many years since I had seen or spoken to him.

"Come to bed," Mark said. "Tomorrow we'll work together to find out how to reach your father. Now you need to sleep."

I went back to bed, knowing tomorrow would be too late.

It was a crisp and clear morning on December 6, 2001. I was stopped at a red light on my way to work when I was overcome with a tingling sensation throughout my body. I was no longer sitting in my car waiting for the traffic light to turn green. My mind had been transported from my body, and

I found myself standing in my father's snow-covered front lawn at his home in Delaware. I watched as he opened the front door of his home. It was very early morning, and I knew that his wife was not yet awake. I also knew that my father had gone through a rough night of little or no sleep. I could see it in his eyes. He was in his slippers and robe and looked almost jaundiced, his eyes yellow with hints of red. He did not see me. He was in pain but wouldn't admit it. As he walked down his front walkway to retrieve his newspaper, he felt the pain in his chest, which had plagued him all night, keeping him awake and afraid of falling sleep. But this pain was tighter than before. It ran through his chest, wrapping around his heart with intensity and refusing to give up until it strangled the last beat from his chest. He fell to the ground, and I watched as he lay in front of his home, alone in the snow. I watched as his spirit left his sickly body. It was over. My chance of reconnecting with him during this lifetime was no more.

At the sound of exasperated drivers honking for me to proceed through the green light, I was brought back to my car and continued my drive to work.

When I returned home late that afternoon, I told Mark, "We'll be getting the call tomorrow."

The phone rang late afternoon the next day, December 7, 2001. I already knew the message. I answered the phone. It was a cousin from my mother's side of the family.

"Hi, it's Barbara. I don't know if you remember me. It's been years."

"I remember you," I said.

"I hate to be calling you with this news," she said, "but I just received a phone call from your father's wife. Your Dad is dead. His wife found him later in the morning, outside, in the front lawn. He was apparently getting the newspaper when he had a massive heart attack and died. She went outside to find him lying in the snow in his robe and slippers, but he was already dead. I'm sorry. She asked me to let his children know."

It had happened just as I had seen it. The man who spent his adult life as a pharmacologist, researching medication for the heart, was now dead from a heart attack.

I had never put much thought into this premonition. I hadn't discussed it with anyone but Mark. But I knew it was important. It was a window into my ability to sense beyond time and space. It led me to his funeral, where the mystery around this man so important to me became both clearer and murkier. The memories were painful.

The turnout for my father's funeral service was very small. This surprised me for a man who had been so well respected in his field of work. The room was sparse, with minimal flowers and no family pictures decorating the walls in celebration of his life. I sat on the metal folding chair with my aunt sitting on one side of me and Mark on the other. My sister sat on the other side of my aunt. We stared at the body lying in the cold, metal casket as the minister began the eulogy. The minister spoke of a man who was an honored Vietnam War vet who was reminded of his bravery every day as he walked with a limp caused by an injury sustained in battle. He spoke of a man who spent years as a professional bowler, winning tournaments around the country. He spoke of a loving man who was a dedicated husband, father, and grandfather.

He spoke of someone who was not my father. Could I possibly be at the wrong service? I looked around the room and again at the man in the coffin. No. That was definitely his wife sitting in the front row and that was definitely my father lying in the coffin.

The minister must have mixed up his notes and read a eulogy written for another person. That had to be the answer. But as I looked at the strangers surrounding me, they were nodding their heads in agreement as the minister spoke. I looked at my sister and my aunt. They looked as confused as I was feeling.

My aunt turned to me and said, "Your father NEVER fought in the Vietnam War. Your father NEVER was a professional bowler! What's going on here?"

My father did enjoy bowling. He owned his own bowling ball and shoes. He took me and my sister bowling during his scheduled visitation shortly after my parent's separation. He spent many hours watching professional bowling on TV. But he was not a professional bowler.

My father did have a limp, caused by an almost fatal car accident when he was a teenager. He had taken his family's uninsured car without permission, after being told not to. He had driven it into a bleak and stormy winter's night and had lost control on a patch of ice on a steep hill. The car had rolled down the hill, away from the road and out of sight. No one saw the accident, and only my father's intelligence saved his life. He luckily remained conscious, made a tourniquet to control his bleeding and managed to crawl up the hill to the road and get help. Multiple surgeries and a pin in his hip left him with a limp. Insurance didn't cover his medical procedures, nearly bankrupting my grandparents.

It was obvious that the man whom I had spied on in my early years, the man who was a mystery to me, was also a mystery to his new wife. She, too, obviously did not truly know my father. Why didn't he tell her the truth about his limp? It had prevented him from serving in Vietnam, and I realized the shame and guilt he must have harbored over this car accident throughout his life. Did his family remind him regularly of his mistake or did his own demons of guilt sabotage his relationships with his family and perhaps himself?

My sister, my aunt, and I were not acknowledged as family during the funeral service. We were not allowed to sit with his wife and her children and receive condolences. No family friends from my childhood attended. No wake was held. Only the brief service was held prior to the burial — a service for my father, a man I did not know.

But I didn't give up on him even then. I had convinced myself that not having a relationship with my father was his loss, not mine. I had convinced myself that my father would show me he loved me by leaving me something in his will. I was sure he somehow knew of my desire to open a school and would leave me the seed money for it. It would be his way of supporting me and letting me know in the end that he really did love me. I felt this was supposed to happen. It felt right. It felt familiar. My father's will would make everything all right.

I paid the fee and requested a copy of his will. I waited each day for the mail to arrive. When it finally came, I opened it with shaking hands. I unfolded the will and began to read. Page one: nothing. Page two: nothing. Page three: nothing. I must have missed it. Read again. Still nothing. My name and my sister's name were nowhere in the will. We were not even mentioned. My father had left everything to his wife and her children. I was numb. My father had left this physical world with no acknowledgement of me.

I had responded to this devastating realization in the same way I had so often dealt with the obstacles and pain in my life. I shook it off. I told myself it didn't matter, that he had missed out on a great love from his daughter. I had gotten this far without him. I knew I would find a way to open my school without him. You can't miss something you never had, right? Life continues. Put a smile on your face. Move on.!

The cold, depressing winter finally ended. More than four months had passed since my father's death. It was a beautiful spring morning. I was in my closet looking for something to wear to work. So many choices. Why was this so difficult? I just needed to get dressed. It shouldn't be this hard. I found my aggravation rising and my anger growing. I began taking clothes off their hangers and throwing the clothes to the floor. I wanted to scream. Why couldn't I find something to wear? I felt the tears of anger falling from my eyes and crawling down my face. I collapsed to the floor of my closet. I opened my eyes to find my husband holding me, concern on his face. I was crying uncontrollably, "I have nothing to wear!" I said over and over. Mark called work and told them I wouldn't be in that day. He dressed me in sweats and a T-shirt. He brought me to bed and had me lie down while he made a few phone calls. Why couldn't I stop crying? My husband took me by the arm and walked me to the car. We drove to a therapist's office. It was time for counseling. It was time to stop lying to myself. Not having a relationship with my father was my loss, too.

We are only as sick as our secrets. I believe that my father had many secrets that I will never know, many secrets that were not only buried deep inside him, but are now buried with him. I don't want to die without doing my best to be honest with myself. To be authentic. To be true to myself. *To thine own self be true*… I had direction. My GPS was set to self-discovery.

Chapter 15: Swimming through the Pain

More learning can occur when there are many obstacles than when there are few or none. A life with difficult relationships, filled with obstacles and losses, presents the most opportunity for the soul's growth. You may have chosen the more difficult life so that you could accelerate your physical progress. — Brian L. Weiss

Once Jennifer was safely on the school bus in the mornings, I couldn't wait to grab my coffee and journal and sit in the rocking chair on my front porch. I found myself savoring the quiet morning as an opportunity to explore my soul through writing. Journaling, for me, was now a needed tool to help me find direction and meaning on my path of self-awareness. The more I wrote, the more I learned and the better I felt. Journaling gave my mind a chance to slow down and digest the circumstances of my life, which was the very thing I had been avoiding for many years. Journaling allowed me to express my true self, without judgment from others.

Since the workshop with Dr. Weiss, a floodgate to my memories had been opened. Using pen and paper, I began swimming through the pain, falseness, and memories of the past, revealing unhealthy patterns and helping me to address my deepest needs. The more I quieted my mind, the more I remembered. The more I remembered, the more I felt the stormy water inside me become tranquil. The more tranquil the water became, the less I needed the dam I had so carefully constructed throughout the years. The more I chiseled away the dam, the more I healed. My hardcover journal was filling to the brim.

The phone rang in the home where I had taken a summer job babysitting for a family who lived across town. Five days a week I would ride my bike to their home to care for their infant son. It was a hot afternoon near the end of August, and I was beginning to anticipate the start of my sophomore year in high school.

As I got up from the couch to answer the phone, I glanced at the clock. It was 4 p.m. My shift ended at 5. I politely answered to an unknown caller, "Hello, Golds' residence."

The curt, brisk voice on the other end of the phone replied.

"It's your mother. Do not make any plans for this evening and do not ride your bike home. I will be there to pick you up at five o'clock."

I knew something was not right.

"Okay," I replied. "But why? What's going on? Is everything alright?"

"Just don't make any plans and be ready to go at five," she said.

"But," I started to respond, but mother had hung up. She said her piece, made her point and was finished. My stomach churned and tightened. My head began to spin. I knew that whatever my mother had planned, it was not going to be good.

It had been a rough four years since my parents separated and divorced. My father had remarried and moved to Delaware, having little or nothing to do with me, which should not have surprised me. I had completed my first year of high school, and my mother was engaged to Sig, a man who was only a year or two younger than her own father. Her fiancé also was an alcoholic who had moved in with us after he lost his license for driving while under the influence. My mother claimed that I was the reason he had too much to drink the night he lost his license. She said he needed to drink to deal with my sullen mood during dinner at the restaurant and my lack of appreciation for him buying me a meal. It was my fault that he now lived with us and that my mother had to drive him to and from work each day.

My mother had met Sig at a Fourth of July party during the summer after my seventh grade. Sig was instantly attracted to my mother and didn't leave her side throughout the entire party. During the car ride home from the festivities, my mother confided to me that Sig had asked her out, but that she had absolutely no interest in him. In fact, she found his aggressive, persistent manner to be overbearing and offensive. I was relieved and didn't give Sig a second thought.

Later that same week I went on vacation with family friends to Cape Cod. When I returned, I was more than shocked to be greeted by my mother and Sig, walking towards me, hand in hand. My mother had spent the week in a whirlwind romance and had apparently decided that blindsiding me was the best way to share the news. I felt a heavy rain begin in my heart and knew it was time to build a dam for protection.

I hated having Sig in our home. I hated how much he influenced my mother. Not only did he drink, he also smoked heavily. Ten years after my mother had stopped smoking, she took up the habit again when she began dating Sig. I had an extremely difficult time accepting my mother's smoking. My father smoked, and she hated it. She hated the way my sister and I smelled after returning from visitation with my father and would immediately put us in the bath to rid us of the stench of cigarette tobacco. But now she didn't seem to care that we smelled of smoke all the time. She said I was also to blame for her smoking. She couldn't handle the stress I caused her.

The drinking began the moment they both got home from work — bourbon with a splash of ginger ale. By the time dinner was finished and my five-year-old sister was put to bed, the effects of the alcohol were obvious. My mother and Sig would sit at the kitchen table, attempting to have conversation with each other as their words slurred and their cigarette ashes tumbled to the kitchen floor. I would close myself in my room, listen to Bruce Springsteen and dream of a time when I would have control of my life, a time when I would be Born To Run. Often, late at night I would descend the stairs and find my mother and Sig fully dressed and passed out at the kitchen table. I lived in fear that they would fall asleep with a lit cigarette and burn the house to the ground. I did my best to stay awake until they fell asleep so I could make sure all cigarettes were extinguished.

My sister, Kathleen, was too young to fully understand what was going on, and Sig embraced her as his own daughter. I, on the other hand, was the rebellious teenager who demanded explanations for their behaviors. Sig often called me a pain in the ass and had threatened to leave my mother because of my unaccepting attitude. He was right. I was unaccepting. The situation did not feel right. It didn't feel healthy. I felt alone. I felt stranded. I was fighting against the current and my mother just could not throw me the life jacket of listening to me and validating my feelings. I was expected to lock up the storm rising inside me, plaster a smile on my face, and live life as if nothing was wrong. But the dam was leaking.

My mother had used physical means to control me since I was a young child. I found myself fighting back. The last physical altercation ended with me kicking my mother in the leg to escape from her restraint. I injured her. I hated what was happening. I didn't want to hurt her, and I was tired of being hurt. I wanted my mother back. I didn't want to live in a storm.

I could see why Sig disliked me. I was either withdrawn and guarded, using my strength to hold back the anger and hurt, or my feelings breached the dam in a torrent and I lashed out in defiance. I often heard Sig declare during his bourbon-enhanced discussions with my mother that they would have such a happy family without me.

"She's the one holding us back, Marie!" he would shout at my mother. "God damn it, Marie, I don't need this. Maybe I should just move out!"

This was a threat I had heard before. I always knew that if Sig was angry, my mother would be angry, and I would bear the brunt of that anger. In addition to the booze, Sig was my mother's mood-altering substance.

This week, Sig had followed through on his threat and had gone back home to stay with his daughters. I had hope for a chance of normalcy, for healing, for reconnecting with my mother. The phone call killed that hope.

I stared at the phone, listening to the dial tone in bewilderment before placing it gently on the receiver. In the distance I heard the sound of the baby crying and realized I had the life of another that needed tending. I fought back the tears and picked the baby up from his crib. He was not quite three months old. It was an overwhelming feeling to know that I was trusted with such a new life. I changed his diaper, warmed his bottle, and settled in on the couch holding him gently in my arms. As I fed him his bottle, our eyes made contact and held a gaze for what seemed like a long time. It was as though this infant was talking to me with his eyes, giving me strength, telling me I was loved. My eyes filled with tears as I looked at this little life before me. In my heart, I knew this would be the last time I saw him. I knew we were saying goodbye.

Shortly after he had sucked the last drop of formula from his bottle, I heard the door to the house open and watched as Mrs. Gold entered. Her face glowed with a warm smile as she took her baby from me and wrapped him in her arms.

"Your mother is parked in front of the house. Is she driving you home today?" Mrs. Gold asked me.

"Yes, she is," I replied.

"Okay then," she stated. "I don't want to keep your mom waiting so we can chat when you get here tomorrow morning."

I hesitated, not wanting to leave, not wanting to face what I feared might be ahead of me. I looked down at the floor and took a deep breath.

"Is everything okay?" Mrs. Gold gently asked.

I lifted up my head and looked her in the eyes.

"Thank you for giving me this job for the summer," I said.

"You don't need to thank me," she said. "I thank you for taking such great care of my baby! We still have a couple weeks left of the summer, and then I hope you'll continue to babysit for us on weekends and other occasions when you aren't in school."

"I would like that," I said. "I better go now. Goodbye."

"See you tomorrow! Have a good night!" I heard Mrs. Gold say before I closed the front door.

My eyes squinted as I walked into the bright sun. I loved the long days of summer and hated that the season was nearing its end. I watched as my mother put my bicycle in the back of the station wagon. I approached the car, opened the front door, and slid quietly into the front seat. I immediately noticed that my sister, Kathleen, was not in the car, which meant someone had to be taking care of her. The car shook as my mother slammed the back door closed, and I held my breath as she sat down in the driver's seat. She said nothing as she put the key in the ignition, started the car, and pulled away from the Golds' home. I swallowed hard and cheerfully asked my mother where we were going.

"Home," she curtly answered.

I was confused.

"Why couldn't I just have ridden my bike home?" I asked. "And where is Kathleen? Why didn't she come with you?"

My mother chose not to acknowledge me, which caused me to become even more concerned and upset. As we drove in silence, I could feel the waves of water pressing on the dam. I closed my eyes and concentrated on strengthening myself.

As my mother pulled the station wagon into the driveway, I noticed an unfamiliar car parked at our house. I quickly opened the car door and ran inside the house to find my mother's father and her Aunt Eileen standing in the kitchen. I turned to see my mother standing behind me. I heard my little sister's feet running down the hallway to greet me. She came into the kitchen smiling, with her arms outstretched for me to hold her. Aunt Eileen quickly scooped up my sister, and my mother directed her to take Kathleen into the bedroom and close the door. I was scared. Then I noticed the suitcase in the corner of the room.

"What's going on?" I said.

"Calm down and watch how you speak," my grandfather ordered as he walked towards me, clearly ready to throw me to the ground and restrain me if needed.

"It's obvious that you are not happy here living with us. You don't want to follow my rules, and you are destroying my relationship with Sig. Therefore, I am sending you to Delaware to live with your father and his wife," my mother explained in an icy tone. "Let them deal with you. Maybe you'll be happier there."

"How am I getting to Delaware?" I asked.

"You're taking a train. Your grandfather and I are driving you to the station. I have a suitcase packed for you, and I'll send you the rest of your things," my mother said.

"What? Does my father know I am coming?" I asked.

"I called your father. He'll meet you at the train station," she said.

"You can't do this!" I screamed. "What about school? What about my job? What about my friends? What about my sister?"

My grandfather shouted, "You are lucky you are not my kid. I would have beaten the hell out of you already. You are lucky to still be alive, you ungrateful whore!"

My head was spinning, and my heart was racing. The dam was about to break. I needed to escape. I quickly opened the kitchen door and ran. I didn't know where I was going, but I ran. I ran up the street and turned my head to see that my grandfather and mother were behind me. I ran faster. I ran to a neighbor's home and screamed for them to please let me in, to please help me. The door opened, and I ran in the house.

"Please stop them! Please don't let them send me away!" I cried.

The front door of the neighbor's home flew open, and there stood my grandfather. He grabbed me by the hair and started to pull me from the home.

"You slut!" He yelled at me. "You are not getting away from us!"

He then let go of my hair, grabbed me by the arms and dragged me from the house into the front lawn where my mother was standing. My grandfather continued holding my arms behind my back while my mother took her hand and hit me back and forth in the face, breaking a tooth. I could taste the chalky bitterness of the tooth as it crumbled onto my tongue. I could feel the warmth of my blood fill my mouth and slowly ooze down my chin, dripping onto my shirt. I had no strength left to fight back.

I could hear the neighbor yelling at my mother to stop and threatening to call the police.

"This is my daughter, and she is none of your business," my mother declared. "I can discipline her as I see fit."

I was beaten. I surrendered. I allowed my mother and grandfather to drag me back to my mother's house, put me in the car with my packed suitcase and drive me to the train station. I spent the car ride looking out the window as tears streamed down my face. Won't someone save me?

We arrived at the train station, and my mother and grandfather immediately walked me to the train platform. On the way to the platform, we saw a man lying on the ground, clutching a bottle wrapped in a brown paper bag as he slept. My mother looked at the man and stopped walking. She took my face in her hand and turned it to the direction of the man passed out on the ground.

"Do you see him?" she yelled at me. "THAT is a drunk! Do you hear me? THAT is a drunk! Remember this man next time you want to call me a drunk!"

It was clear to me at this point that I was swimming alone against a strong current of denial. I was dangerous. I was rocking my mother's boat. My mother was afraid she might fall off the boat she had so carefully constructed and have to learn to swim in the water she had been avoiding for years.

The train arrived. My mother and grandfather stayed, not to say goodbye, but to ensure that I was on that train as it pulled away from the station. I boarded the train, went directly to the bathroom and washed the blood from my face. As I exited the bathroom, I took a deep breath and found a seat in the least crowded train car. I sat alone with my head buried in my hands while I cried all the way to Delaware.

"Next stop, Newark, Delaware!" I heard the conductor announce.

I lifted my head and wiped my eyes. The train stopped, and I found my father and his wife waiting for me on the platform. I had hoped my father would take me in his arms and hold me, telling me everything would be all right. Instead, he and his wife stood there smiling, politely saying hello. My father took my suitcase, and I followed him to the car. We rode to my father's house in silence. I was brought upstairs and shown to my room. It was empty, with a pillow and some blankets on the hardwood floor.

"We'll go out and buy you a mattress tomorrow," my father said. Then he turned, left the room and went downstairs to his wife.

The door to my room remained opened, and I could hear my father and his wife talking.

"Why would she do this to us?" my stepmother asked in a shaky voice. "Why can't your ex-wife just leave us alone? She's so jealous of our relationship and has only sent your daughter here to live with us in an attempt to break up our marriage. I don't want her here!"

"I know, baby" my father said in a soothing voice. "Marie has always been very jealous, and this is just one of her attempts to get me back in her life. It won't work. I am yours. Trust me, I didn't ask for this and don't like it any more than you do!"

The loving way in which my father spoke to his new wife was unrecognizable to me. I was sent to live in a house of strangers. I closed my door, sat on the floor of my new, empty room, and put my face in the pillow. It was time to bail before I drowned. I was swimming in a sea of crazy and had to put all my energy into surviving.

Before I drifted off to sleep, I reminded myself to call the Golds first thing in the morning to let them know I would no longer be able to babysit.

Chapter 16: Introducing Emelyn

Soulful relationships bring true joy into our lives. — Dr. Brian Weiss

The crisp cool air of fall was fading. The temperature had dropped, and the once beautiful leaves lay brown and dried on the ground, exposing the bare limbs of the trees. The blue skies of October had turned into the dull gray of November. Tracey and I were once again leaving for Savannah, and I was packing both spring and fall clothes into my suitcase, not sure what the weather would be like this time of the year. It was a week before Thanksgiving, but we would be returning to our families for the holiday. Tracey and I wanted to uncover the history of *The House.* I was determined to research the lineage of owners in hopes of putting a name to the woman who had come to me in my regressions.

I was definitely leaving the city of my comfort to explore unknown territory. Ever since I had found *The House* during our last trip to Savannah, it had been difficult for me to concentrate on anything else. I needed to find answers. Once again we would stay at the Eliza Thompson House within walking distance of *The House* and the Georgia Historical Society, where we would do our research.

The staff at Eliza Thompson greeted us warmly and showed us to our room on the lower level with its own entrance on Jones Street. I flopped on my bed, exhausted from the day's travels and my lack of sleep from the excitement and anticipation the night before. I watched as Tracey carefully unpacked her suitcase, gently placing her clothes on hangers in the closet. I had no desire to unpack just yet and was perfectly content, lying on the bed of this historic room, taking in my surroundings and enjoying the sweet smell of the live oak trees just outside the window. Something inside me changes whenever I reach Savannah. It's where I feel the most authentic and relaxed. It's where I feel at home.

Once Tracey finished unpacking, we grabbed our sweaters and cameras and headed out for a walk along Jones Street. We leisurely strolled along the brick street, enjoying the late evening air, stopping to take random pictures of obscure things. We pointed our camera at the tops of the oak trees and snapped pictures. We took pictures of houses, buildings, parking lots, and the sky. We took pictures of the ground, the sidewalk, and street signs. We just kept pressing the button on the camera, not focused on the subject matter. When we returned to our room, we sat and studied the pictures we had taken, amazed by the number of orbs of all shapes, sizes and colors captured in our photos.

After spending some time chatting and speculating as to whether some of these orbs were actually "spirits," we decided it was time to call it a night. We needed to rest and focus on what we came here to do. Tomorrow we were going to the Historical Society to try to solve the mysteries of our past life regressions by uncovering more pieces to the puzzle. I was determined to find who lived in the corners of my memory, sharing a story that seemed all too familiar.

The Savannah branch of the Georgia Historical Society sits on the corner of Gaston and Whitaker streets, across from Forsyth Park and a short walk from the Eliza Thompson House. The Historical Society is housed in Hodgson Hall, a building that was a gift of Margaret Telfair Hodgson and her sister Mary Telfair as a memorial to Margaret's husband, William B. Hodgson, a prominent Savannah citizen, American diplomat, and oriental scholar. Architect Detlef Lienau designed the headquarters building, which was completed in 1876. The society, incorporated in 1839, holds the world's largest collection of materials dealing with Georgia history. If we were to find any answers to our questions, they would be found here.

As we entered the grand building of the Historical Society, I was in awe of the books and materials that lined the walls of this open, two-story building. I was taken aback by the overwhelming appreciation I had for the beautiful architecture and rich history that was held in the walls of this magnificent mansion.

I stood in the entryway, wide-eyed with my mouth gaping, and I turned to Tracey only to discover that she had already made her way to the front desk. I quickly followed, registered at the desk, handed in my purse, and signed a paper agreeing to obey the rules of the Historical Society.

Now where to begin? We decided to start by researching *The House* — the antique store I had so clearly experienced in a regression. We gave the woman behind the desk the address of the house and asked her how we could find the records for it. We wanted to learn the names of the families who had owned it through the years.

The woman brought us to the correct section and explained the process of requesting any materials stored in the archives. Archived materials had to be viewed at designated tables, and white gloves had to be worn when touching photos or other fragile items. Tracey and I wasted no time researching maps, records, and deeds to the home. It wasn't long before we confirmed what we had learned during our prior visit from the young woman who worked in Alex Raskin's antiques. General Hardee started building the mansion prior to the Civil War and unfortunately passed away before its completion. When the home was finished during the Reconstruction era in the 1870s, a lack of money forced the builders to convert the mansion to a two-family home.

Further research of the chain of title showed that in 1870 Ann Hardee sold the home to Algernon S. Hartridge. He moved his family from his Jones Street property to the new home on Monterey Square, and the family owned the home until the death Mrs. Hartridge in 1885. It was then sold to E.A. Weil, who restored it to a single-family home and owned it until 1912. During the 1870s until the early 1900s, the Noble Hardee Mansion became one of the city's most sophisticated mansions, playing host to many important social gatherings.

The time period when the Hartridge family owned the home seemed to correlate to the time period of my regression. It would also explain why I remembered the wall next to the sprawling staircase as the end of the home. The building had been a two-family structure then.

While I was still researching the background of the Hardee mansion, Tracey went to the computers and began researching the Hartridge family. It wasn't long before I felt Tracey tugging at my arm. I stopped reading to look up at her. With a sparkle in her eyes and excitement in her voice, Tracey said, "I found you! I found you!"

"What are you talking about?" I replied in a whisper.

"Come over to the computer," Tracey said. "You have to read this. I found an article about a woman from the Hartridge family. When I read the article I thought I was reading about you! You have to see it! It's as though they're writing about you in the article! Come see!"

I held my breath until I reached the computer and let out a sigh in disbelief as I read the article. As much as logic wanted to tell me that this could not be, my inner compass pointed me toward embracing the possibility that this was the woman who appeared in my regression.

I stared at the computer screen and reread the article. It was an obituary printed in the *Savannah Morning News* dated Saturday, September 26, 1942. The headline read, Miss Hartridge Dies in New York.

Miss Emelyn Battersby Hartridge, former Savannahian and distinguished educator, died Thursday at her residence in New York. She had been living in New York since her retirement from active work in the educational field. Only a few months ago, Miss Hartridge visited Savannah for some weeks and renewed her many personal friendships and connections.

Miss Hartridge was the eldest daughter of the late Alfred Lamar Hartridge and Julia Smythe (Wayne) Hartridge. She was born July 17, 1871, in Savannah.

I paused to think for a minute. I clearly remembered experiencing the death of a woman during a past life regression. Yes, it was clear in the regression that the woman was an educator who had recently retired. It was also clear that it was September and she was reflecting on the start of a new school year. I also clearly remembered that the woman in my regression was living in a city far from her original home. I remembered feeling that the city was New York. Coincidence?

Miss Hartridge was a woman of unusually fine intellect and many gifts. She was graduated from Vassar in 1892. Founding the Hartridge School in Savannah in 1892, she took the leadership in educational work here for a number of years and was widely recognized as a woman of intellectual and scholarly attainments. She left Savannah in 1903 to become principal of the Hartridge School in Plainfield, New Jersey.

What? Miss Emelyn Hartridge founded her own school in Savannah and ended up moving to New Jersey to be principal of a school she named after herself? Is it another coincidence that I live in New Jersey and have always felt as though I was not only an educator, but a school founder? Is it any coincidence that although I have lived practically my entire life in New Jersey, I feel at home in Savannah? Could I have picked up where Miss Hartridge left off? Or have I been desperately attempting to recreate a life that I have already experienced? Am I recreating what feels comfortable and what I know, instead of exploring other options?

My head was spinning. I attempted to discredit what I was feeling. I looked at Tracey and shrugged.

"Oh, I don't think that's the woman I'm experiencing in my regressions. Just because she was an educator and opened her own school doesn't make her me. Plus the picture of her looks nothing like me."

I scrutinized the photo printed with the obituary. The older woman had her graying hair neatly pulled back in a bun. Her face appeared a bit stern, yet softened by a slight smile. However, Miss Emelyn Hartridge did look like the retired woman I saw dying in her bed in her New York City apartment.

"You can't go by the picture!" Tracey argued. "I know this is you. I feel it. Not to mention that her family owned *The House!* They owned *The House* during the time period of your regressions! You can't deny the evidence!"

Evidence. Isn't that what I was looking for? Evidence to support the out-of-ordinary experiences of Dr. Weiss' workshop? Is the information presented before me proof that the woman in my regression really did exist? Was this enough evidence to satisfy my rational mind? Would my ego be silenced? A force was leading me on a magical adventure. A force that allowed me to deliver a message to a woman in need at Dr. Weiss' workshop. Although I relayed to her the words from her husband she was so desperately longing to hear, the message did not come from me. I was only the vessel being used to deliver a life-saving message, one that came from a force far greater than anything in the physical realm. It was the same force that led me on my past-life journey. It was an energy force of pure light and love. It was a force that is life-changing. It was a force that is life-saving.

The woman who had received my psychic/medium reading at Dr. Weiss' workshop came to me a stranger, but after receiving her message, I felt connected to her soul. I knew it was a connection that would last an eternity, even though I also knew I would probably never see her again.

At the same workshop, the woman who had come to me in a past-life regression was a stranger to me in this physical world, yet I could feel her soul. I felt connected to her on a different plane. I knew that if I allowed her to lead me, she would guide me on my journey of self-discovery.

Perhaps Tracey was right. One can't deny evidence, and that's what I needed. I decided to research Emelyn Battersby Hartridge and her family to prove to myself that my regression experiences were accurate. If I couldn't find the proof, I would drop this whole insane notion.

I squirmed and bit my lip as I tried to muffle the voice inside that said, *"Ah, still not ready to trust your intuition? We have work to do!"*

Chapter 17: No More Hiding

The past is over, the future not yet here. Learn from the past and let it go. Plan for the future, but don't worry. Only then can you truly enjoy the present. —*Dr. Brian Weiss*

I returned from Savannah a few days before Thanksgiving. I was preparing the meal this year, and for the first time in a long while, I found myself taking pleasure in the task. Over the years, I had found these same duties mundane and an interruption to what was really important (work!). Today, I sincerely enjoyed creating the menu, decorating the house, reading through recipes, and cooking with my family. It felt like a gift. I was present, not only physically, but mentally.

While working in the kitchen with my husband, son and daughter, I found that I was singing along to the music that was playing as we were chopping celery, slicing potatoes, and putting pies in the oven. The usual stressful anticipation of my mother and sister coming to my home was not there. I felt calm and at peace. When hosting or attending a family function, I had been accustomed to my mind becoming preoccupied with thoughts of past family events. I would begin to analyze the arguments, criticisms, and unspoken tension that seemed to stifle the room. I then proceeded to role-play in my mind how the gathering would unfold and how I would handle the situation. By the time I was actually with my family, I was anxious and in defense mode from licking past unhealed wounds and projecting my own feelings of inadequacy during the scheduled event. All this preconceived worry blocked me from finding the good or appreciating the moment. Today was different. I was not criticizing myself. I was not judging how things "should" be. I was not afraid of being judged by my family. I was not hiding behind my wall of protection. I was content with things just as they were.

When my family arrived, I was ready. I wasn't running around like a nut trying to complete last-minute details. I was relaxed. I was prepared. I was genuinely happy to have my family together in the warmth of my home. I felt thankful. My sister pulled me aside while the other family members were enjoying appetizers and conversation.

"There's something different about you," Kathleen said. "Maybe it's because you aren't working, but you seem so relaxed, and I love all the creative expression you brought to this holiday — the beautiful menu you printed, the lovely table setting, not to mention all the delicious food you prepared. I really appreciate the hard work you put into this day! This break in work has allowed you to explore another side of yourself. Thank you!"

Kathleen embraced me and returned to the family room to join the others. I was feeling different, and my sister noticed.

My sister's words meant a lot to me. What she didn't realize was that I had been using all my creativity for the past twenty years in my school and with my students. What I didn't realize was I had not been sharing that side of myself with my family. When I was around my mother, I became a scared child, fearful of being judged, fearful to trust, fearful to just be. The dam I had built was still in place, especially around my family. I had built it to protect me, to help me feel safe. I now realized it was blocking me. It was blocking me from accepting my mother for who she is and loving her at her level, not at the level of my expectations. It was blocking the real me from being present and not allowing the soul connections I wanted to make.

Perhaps I had created a role as the victim by holding on to past judgments and fears. Perhaps being a victim of the past had created a mindset that compromised my self-confidence and self-trust. For me to release the past's hold, I needed destroy the dam and let the water flow. I needed to continue remembering and releasing painful childhood memories. I needed to commit to never allowing myself to become so busy that I no longer took time to quiet my mind and listen to my voice, to heal my inner child.

My first inclination after my school closed was to send out my resume and find work. I had always worked, so not having a full-time job felt foreign to me. However, nothing I applied for seemed to work out. This was also foreign to me. I realized that I was older and experienced and at the top of the pay scale, but this was different. The more resumes I sent out, the stronger I felt that this was not the direction I should be taking. I was not supposed to fall back into the same old pattern. My inner voice kept telling me that I had the experience at Dr. Weiss' workshop for a reason. It was a gift. I was not to overlook this gift. I was to take the time to explore it and nurture it. I was not to force things to happen. I was to trust and let things happen. I felt that to fulfill my higher life purpose, I needed to follow through with what my inner guidance was telling me. If I pursued yet another job in public education, I would not find my higher purpose and would live in regret. Financially, it would be difficult, but I needed to let go of ego-guided attachments and trust the guidance of spirit.

It was that Thanksgiving Day that I made the commitment to trust. I would do my best not to question or go against my inner voice. I now knew what it was like to connect on a soul level. I wanted to be in touch with my soul. I wanted to know who I really am and move forward.

I believe spirit had guided me to the opening of my school. I also believe spirit guided me to the closing of it. It was time to exercise my intuition back into shape. It was time to commit to being present. It was time to learn how to live as if I have nothing to hide.

Chapter 18: History Repeats Itself

You will not find happiness by changing things outside of yourself. —Dr. Brian Weiss

As much as I had enjoyed spending time with my family over the holidays, Emelyn Hartridge remained forefront in my thoughts. I was so intrigued to learn that she founded a private school in Savannah. What made her take on such an undertaking? Did she have help? Why did she leave her school to work as a principal in New Jersey? I needed to find answers to these questions.

As a child, I felt that education and owning a school was somehow in my DNA, but the focus of my school became clear my sophomore year in high school after I left my father's home in Delaware to live once again with my mother.

Less than two months after putting me on a train to Delaware, my mother and Sig were married. I was not there to question, complain, or rebel against their decision, which gave them the freedom to begin their new life. Both my parents had found new lives, and I did not feel included in either. I was alone, navigating the torrential tides of crazy, relying on my internal compass to lead the way.

I sat alone on the school bus staring at the window, watching the drops of rain slowly trickle down the glass. The dark, cold November weather seemed to represent my feelings. The Delaware teachers strike had ended last week, and I had begun my sophomore year of high school, treading in a sea of unknown territory without the support of family or friends.

Although I had longed for school and a sense of normalcy during the two-month strike, I now wished that the strike would go on without end. This year, Delaware had been court ordered to desegregate its school districts by busing students from the predominantly inner city schools to predominantly white suburban districts and vice versa. I overheard my father say that many white families were sending their children to private schools or moving out of state. I found it hard to believe that the year 1980 was approaching and situations such as this still occurred. My first week of school I found myself hiding in the bathrooms to escape the tension and fighting in almost every corner of the building. Students did not return to well-rested teachers eagerly awaiting the new year. The resentment and anger permeated the air. I had no safe place to call my own.

The first-period bell rang. Lockers slammed, and I could hear the sounds of students running to class. I sat silently at my desk doodling on my spiral notebook, attempting to make myself as small as possible, hoping not to be seen. As students came piling into the room, I kept my eyes down, avoiding human contact.

"Good morning! Excuse me! I need your attention, please!"

The confident female voice coming from the front of the classroom did not belong to Mr. my first-period teacher. From the corner of my eye I could see him sitting at his desk, reading the newspaper. His eyes did not leave the paper held by his thick, rough fingers with nails bitten to the quick. His bulging body was much like his ego, inflated and coarse. The ex-football player, now coach, had better things to do than engage a classroom of non-athletes. It was obvious that he had no intention of acknowledging the woman standing in front of the room.

I allowed my eyes to look away from my notebook and at the woman smiling sincerely, while patiently waiting for the students to settle down. Her light blue suit jacket was left unbuttoned, exposing a shirt adorned with pastel flowers. The small heels of her wedged shoes peeked out from under her cream colored pants. Her look was professional, yet practical. Her tone was assertive, yet approachable.

"Good morning," the woman said with authority, signaling the students to close their mouths and actually look at her. "My name is Mrs. Cloud, and I am the school's crisis counselor."

Mrs. Cloud used her small hands and short fingers that ended in clear polished nails to brush her brown curls away from her forehead before she continued.

"Like many of you, this is my first year at the school, and I'm learning my way as well. I would like us to learn and grow together. Although I have the word "crisis" in my title, you do not need to have a crisis in order to come speak with me. I am willing to listen and support in any way possible. Our visits are considered confidential, and my office is located in the guidance department. Please feel free to come see me any time."

Still smiling, she picked up her briefcase and walked out of the class on her wedge-heeled shoes.

Throughout the morning, I couldn't stop thinking about Mrs. Cloud and how sincere she seemed. I had suffered for months without the guidance of an adult. Could Mrs. Cloud offer the guidance I was craving? That afternoon I found the courage to go to her office. That afternoon I found my safe place with Mrs. Cloud.

Mrs. Cloud and I met regularly. Her sincerity and non-judgmental approach allowed me to share with her how I ended up living in Delaware and how unhappy I was.

When Mrs. Cloud asked, I agreed to let her speak with my parents. She said it was important to include them in my healing process. I gave her their phone numbers.

Mrs. Cloud contacted my mother, who was willing to talk. Mrs. Cloud called my father. He was not as receptive. There was nothing wrong with him. He didn't need to speak to Mrs. Cloud. It had to be clear to her that I was the problem, not him. Don't call him again.

The day Mrs. Cloud contacted my Dad was the night he stormed into my room. It was the night he pushed me onto my mattress, using his nicotine stained fingers to tear the cross necklace from my neck, leaving long, bloody scratches from his unkempt nails running from my neck to my chest, and a broken gold chain on the wooden floor of my nearly empty room. The anger glared from his eyes as he looked through me. The sight of me shaking and hurt seemed to amuse him, much as our cowering family dog had made him laugh

He laughed as he asked, "Did you think I really wanted you here? Did you? I never wanted you. Never." He continued laughing as he left my room. I locked the door behind him.

The next morning I went straight to Mrs. Cloud's office. My wounds were now visible. Mrs. Cloud immediately called my mother, acting as a mediator, to work out an agreeable plan for me to return to my mother's home. I spent all day with Mrs. Cloud as we worked with my mother arranging for my return to New Jersey. My mother set conditions for my return. I had to accept Sig as her husband, follow all of her rules, meet with my school guidance counselor once a week to assess my progress, and understand that my room had been given to my sister, so I would be staying in the guest room until the situation was straightened out. I agreed.

My father's wife drove me to the destination in silence and left me at the station. I stood alone on the platform waiting for the train, hoping this would be my last ride on this route. I didn't have gloves, so I kept my hands in my coat pockets, protecting them from the December wind.

The train that would leave for New Jersey arrived at the Delaware station on time, decorated with cardboard Santa faces taped to the windows and gold tinsel draped around the interior car doors. I boarded the train with same suitcase I had when I arrived to Delaware and nothing else. I would be back in New Jersey in time for Christmas, in time to start the second marking period of school. I was leaving without my father saying goodbye or wishing me well. We hadn't spoken since that night in my room.

I returned to New Jersey to a mother with a new last name and a man who was officially my stepfather. To a house that had been redecorated and to a bedroom that was no longer mine. To a sister I loved and missed, a school I was familiar with, and friends who knew and supported me. I returned.

My guidance counselor – I'll call him Mr. Scarborough — was a small, thin man, with thick greasy dark hair parted to the side. His glasses were just as thick, with thick, black frames to match. His suit jacket was always a size too big, making his small frame appear even smaller.

My presence seemed to make Mr. Scarborough nervous. I don't think he was accustomed to having a regularly scheduled visitor, and he didn't seem to know quite what to do with me.

I entered his office, and he nodded to a chair opposite his desk. As I took my seat in the appropriate chair, Mr. Scarborough nervously cleared his throat and took a seat behind his desk. It was obvious that the desk acted as a protective barrier for Mr. Scarborough, allowing him to fidget with the stapler or ruffle through the mounds of paperwork piled on his desk instead of making eye contact with me.

"So, how are things going? Have you adjusted to your classes?"

It was the same question he had been asking me since my return to New Jersey three weeks ago.

"My classes are too easy, and I'm bored." It was basically the same answer I had given last week and the week before last.

"I have already explained this to you," Mr. Scarborough said. "You were placed in the lower level 'C' classes because you missed the first marking period of school. We thought that these lower level classes would make it easier for you to transition back to school." By "we" he meant him and my mother.

"Okay," I said. "But I already know all the information being taught in these classes. My friends are not in these classes, and I feel like I'm falling behind. I feel unmotivated because I know I can pass without even trying. Couldn't you please at least put me in a higher level English class?"

Mr. Scarborough wiped his brow, adjusted his glasses, and let out an exasperated sigh.

"I am not changing your classes. It is clear to me that you just want to be with your friends. Your mother discussed her concerns with me about you putting your emphasis on your looks, your friends, and not on your schoolwork. How long do you think you can get by in class by being the pretty, popular girl? Have you thought about college? Looking pretty and being with your friends are not going to get you into college. Try applying yourself. Try contributing to class discussions. Try getting A's in all these easy classes and then we'll talk!"

I could see the perspiration building on his brow as Mr. Scarborough continued to tell me how he was all too familiar with my type of student.

"Looks and popularity end, you know. Spend more time studying and putting effort into your work and think about what I have said!"

He stood and handed me a pass to my Home Economics class. I guess this session was over.

As I closed his office door behind me, I quickly wiped the tear that had escaped from my eye and was slowly rolling down my cheek. I was not some shallow girl who only cared about looks and popularity. I loved English class, but the one I was currently in was reading a novel I had read two years ago. Why had Mr. Scarborough not heard me? He obviously had been speaking with my mother, and it was clear that neither one of them knew the real me.

"Late again?" the Home Economics teacher bellowed as I opened the door and entered the class.

All eyes were upon me as I walked to the front of the classroom and handed my late pass to the teacher I'll call Mrs. Drake. I kept my gaze towards the floor and didn't say a word as I tried to quietly join the class without creating a disruption.

"Late again?" Mrs. Drake repeated, only this time she screamed it so loudly that every student stopped working to see why Mrs. Drake was yelling.

All eyes were on me. I felt the acid in my stomach gurgle as a sharp pain entered my chest.

Mrs. Drake's large face was crimson, and her unkempt bangs looked plastered to her forehead as she bellowed, "Is there something wrong with you?"

I stood dumbstruck in the front of the classroom.

"No," I managed to whisper.

"Then why are you always coming from the counselor's office? If you don't have a problem, you wouldn't be going there. So, what is your problem?" she demanded.

I felt humiliated as the class waited for me to answer. The sea inside me was experiencing high tide, and it took all my strength to ride the waves and not fight against the current.

"I don't have a problem," I answered. "Mr. Scarborough wants me to check in with him weekly. He made the schedule."

"Well, you must have major problems or be in some sort of trouble for Mr. Scarborough to want to see you weekly. You tell Mr. Scarborough that if he wants to see you to find another time to do it. Got it?" Mrs. Drake said with a sneer.

"Perhaps you should tell him yourself," I calmly stated as I turned to walk to my workstation.

"Get this straight, young lady. Show up late again, and you fail this class. I don't care if you have problems. The world doesn't care if you have problems. All I care about is that you show up on time to my class. Got it?"

I got it. It was that day as I sat at my workstation and took out my sewing project that I made the commitment to create a school where the staff is dedicated to the whole student. To create a school environment that did care about a student's problems. A school that helped resolve students' issues. A school that gave a crap. A school that provided a supportive community of caring. I decided when I grew up I was going to open a special school. It was going to be a school for students who needed help surviving in an emotional hell. It would be a school that provided life jackets to teenagers swimming in a pool of crazy.

The bell rang. I walked to the storage cabinet to put my project away. Mrs. Drake squeezed her rotund body through the path of classroom tables and stood next to me. I couldn't look at her.

In a much softer tone than before she said, "I am here after school on Tuesdays and Thursdays coaching the cheerleaders. If you ever want to stay after on of those days to work on your project, let me know."

"Thank you," I whispered and walked out the door.

I never took her up on the offer.

Chapter 19: The Story Unfolds

A journey is like marriage. The certain way to be wrong is to think you control it. —Author John Steinbeck (1902–1968)

The bustle of the holidays was over. Winter was here, and I was aching to return to Savannah and the Historical Society. I needed to get better acquainted with Miss Emelyn Battersby Hartridge. I needed to learn more about her family, her school, her life. I needed more proof.

In January I planned my return to Savannah. The cost of airfare prohibited me from flying, so I decided to drive. I also decided to stay only two days at the Eliza Thompson and the rest of the week in Hilton Head, South Carolina, at my family's timeshare. It would be about a fifty-minute drive from Hilton Head to Savannah.

I asked Tracey to join me, and she agreed. She had been feeling discouraged after our last trip. Tracey felt strongly that I had found a personal connection to Emelyn Hartridge, yet she had not found the person she experienced in her regression. We both felt there was a story waiting to be told, but Tracey didn't feel the pieces to her puzzle were falling into place. We hoped she would find what she was looking for during this trip.

The feeling of returning home once I arrived in Savannah increased with each trip. Something about Savannah allowed me to feel at peace.

Tracey and I wasted no time returning to the Historical Society. This time we knew where to begin and went right to the section that contained the information about the Hartridge family. Walter

Charlton Hartridge Jr. created a collection of family photographs, prints, account books, diaries, journals, research notes, organizational records, abstracts from public and church records, legal documents, newspaper and magazine articles, and scrapbooks dating from the 1500s through the 1900s. He gave this collection to the Georgia Historical Society. I filled out the request forms for documents and scrapbooks pertaining to Emelyn Battersby Hartridge's family. The woman working at the desk disappeared to the archives to retrieve my boxes of information.

I sat at the assigned table, put on the white gloves, and held my breath in anticipation of what I might find. Was Emelyn the woman who came to me during my regressions? Would I find any documentation in support of the memories I so vividly experienced? I took a deep breath, bit the side of my cheek and waited for the woman to appear with the information that I hoped would answer my questions.

I watched as the woman returned from the private area of the Historical Society, pushing the cart stacked with my boxes. Her glasses slid down her nose as she carefully placed the boxes behind the front desk. Her plain white sneakers made no sound as she walked towards me holding a box in hand. She placed the box in front of me and pointed to slips of paper and pencils neatly stacked on the table that I could use to take notes. Her voice was assertive as she explained that I would be given one box at a time. When I was finished reviewing a box, I was to return it to the main desk where I would be given another. I quietly nodded my head in agreement, afraid that any sound from my voice would have given away my anxiety.

My gloved fingers slowly opened the treasure sitting in front of me. My body tingled as I read handwritten letters and documents created by Emelyn and members of her family. I was holding history in my hands. I was holding energy shared by people who were once on this physical plane. The enormous amount of respect and reverence I felt while reading intimate words shared among family members left me humbled.

Throughout the week, I continued my research. The more I read the handwritten words from so long ago, the more my thoughts wandered. I found myself creating scenarios of the dialogue between Emelyn and her family. I took liberties with my imagination, allowing myself to watch a movie in my mind.

"Emelyn, please try to understand! It really is what is best for everyone. This situation is too much for your mother to handle right now."

"STEPmother!" Emelyn quickly corrected her father as she continued to sit at the edge of her bed, staring out the window, refusing to look her father in the eye. The decision had been made. Emelyn knew there was no use trying to persuade him.

Emelyn was his firstborn daughter and had a special place in her father's heart. Her headstrong personality, high expectations, and determination were qualities Mr. Hartridge admired and respected. They were the same qualities he possessed. It was these same qualities that allowed Mr. Hartridge to be one of Savannah's most respected war veterans and businessmen.

"Now, Emelyn, you know this is not a permanent arrangement. You and your sister will be home for the holidays. Before you know it, you both will be back home in Savannah," Mr. Hartridge explained.

Emelyn sighed. She knew how important education was to her family. Emelyn's father felt strongly that the males and females of the family needed an education of the highest standard. Until now, Emelyn had been taught at home by governesses. Although Emelyn did not like the idea of having to leave her home, her family and the comfort of Savannah, a city she knew better than the back of her own hand, she knew that attending Vassar Prep was a privilege. She just wished it wasn't so far from home. She also wished the circumstances had been different.

Yes, it was true. Her father's new wife could not handle the situation. After all, she was younger than Emelyn's own brothers. She was thirty years younger than Emelyn's father and more of a contemporary to Emelyn than a maternal figure.

Emelyn had always viewed her position as the oldest daughter in the family seriously. Since her mother's passing, Emelyn had taken over as full-time caregiver and educator to her younger siblings. Even before her mother became ill, Emelyn had a maternal instinct towards them. She naturally cared for them while providing the structure and discipline that was necessary to run a successful home. Emelyn's siblings loved and respected her.

When their mother passed away, it was only natural that Emelyn, at the age of thirteen, became the mother figure, the woman of the house, a title that now threatened Mr. Alfred Lamar Hartridge's new wife, Mary Agnes. Mary Agnes struggled to take control over the Hartridge children. Being a mother to girls who were not much younger than herself was a job she was not ready to undertake, and sharing her role as the woman of the house was not something she was willing to do.

Therefore, the decision had been made. Emelyn would go to boarding school while her younger sister Katherine would live with relatives in North Georgia. Katherine was a bit more outspoken and rebellious when it came to Mr. Hartridge's new marriage, so sending her to live with relatives would allow the new Mrs. Hartridge an opportunity to gain respect from the other children. Having Emelyn away at boarding school would allow the new Mrs. Hartridge to cement her role as the woman of the house.

The records in the Hartridge family boxes showed that Emelyn's mother, Julia Smythe Wayne, had been just a year younger than Emelyn's father. She was a beautiful woman from a prominent, land-owning Savannah family, with ties to Scotland royalty, sea captains, war heroes, well-known public figures, and even pirates.

It was no coincidence that Julia Smythe Wayne married Alfred Lamar Hartridge. The Hartridges were originally from Kent, England. They were a well-respected family with strong roots in Savannah and a lineage of war veterans, lawyers, bankers, and business owners. The merging of the Smythe Wayne and Hartridge families created a powerhouse union that came with many responsibilities and expectations.

It was expected that a family of such high standing as the Hartridges would do a great deal of entertaining, especially for influential and powerful families. Julia Smythe Wayne Hartridge was not a novice when it came to entertaining. She was a descendant of a family who owned Ossabaw Island and the plantations within. Her family was actively associated with public affairs, and entertaining was part of their civic duty. Julia grew up accepting entertaining as part of a wife's role.

In 1871, the year Emelyn was born, Alfred Lamar bought a beautiful large Victorian home along the Vernon River in Beaulieu. In 1872, he moved his family from Savannah to their country home in Beaulieu. Although Beaulieu became the family's main home, the Hartridges continued to split their time between Beaulieu and Savannah. Alfred Lamar owned multiple properties, and Emelyn had many aunts, uncles, and cousins who lived in Savannah, so Emelyn's family visited Savannah often.

Having places to stay throughout Savannah proved to be a useful and necessary blessing for Alfred Lamar's family, seeing that he had to rebuild the family's Beaulieu home three times due to fire. The first fire occurred on July 4, 1875, from a gasoline leak. Less than two years later on January 1, 1877, Alfred Lamar got out of bed to administer medicine to one of his children who was ill. His wife Julia awoke and smelled something burning. The house was once again on fire. Alfred and Julia quickly gathered their children and narrowly escaped the blazing building. The family stood in the cold January air, huddling against one another as they watched the flames once again engulf the structure they called home. It was determined that the second fire was caused by matches ignited by the scratching of rats in the storeroom.

The third fire strangely enough occurred about two years after the second one. A woman living at Beaulieu was distilling liquor in her home. Not wanting any neighbors, she deliberately burned down homes in the area. These fires were only setbacks to Alfred Lamar Hartridge, as he continued to rebuild his Beaulieu home after each fire, determined to maintain the country dwelling for his family.

The Beaulieu home was perfect for the frequent entertaining required by a family of the Hartridges' stature. Julia Hartridge's career was to socialize and entertain. She needed to ensure the family's standing on the social ladder. It was a full-time job. Attending afternoon teas and luncheons, planning parties and dinners, organizing the house staff and keeping up with correspondence took up the majority of Julia's time. As with most influential families, the children were tended to by a governess and house staff, allowing Julia to manage her social obligations.

There was not much information about how Julia Hartridge died. The date, time, and place of her death were recorded, but I found no information explaining the cause. I closed my eyes, picturing Julia in my mind, creating her death the way I imagined, the way I felt it.

When not planning or attending social events, Julia Hartridge took to her bed. With the drapes pulled, a bowl of cool water, ice, and a washrag on the night table, Julia would lie engulfed in the darkness and quiet that became her sanctuary. The children knew not to disturb their mother during her quiet time. When not busied by their studies, the children entertained themselves by running through the spacious house playing hide and seek, or swimming in the Vernon River that ran behind their home.

"Pull it tighter!" Julia Hartridge insisted as one of the house staff women tugged at the corset strings.

"Yes, ma'am. I will do my best."

Watching her mother dress for a social affair fascinated Emelyn. It seemed to be such an agonizing process, and Emelyn found it difficult to understand why women put themselves through such an ordeal. The finished product was always pristine. Her mother's long hair was put up in beautiful combs, and her dress perfectly hugged her cinched waist, making Emelyn worry that her mother would have to hold her breath throughout the whole event. Emelyn enjoyed helping her mom pick out the perfect pieces of jewelry to complete the ensemble. She watched as her mother applied just the right amount of face powder, rouge, and lip color, while examining her work in the vanity mirror. Looking your best was important. It was part of the job.

Emelyn loved watching, from a distance, the dinner parties hosted by her parents. These events were not to be shared with children, but Emelyn would take any opportunity to sneak a peek at the adult dining affair. The dining room table was always set with the best china, crystal, and silver. The house staff spent hours polishing, cleaning and preparing for the dinner.

"Child! Stop spying on the grown folk!" Mammy exclaimed as she put a hand on Emelyn's shoulder and directed her up the stairs to join her sisters. "You need to set the example for your sisters, and the last thing we need is to have six eyes staring at the grown folk while they tryin' to eat!"

Emelyn stomped her feet as she retreated up the stairs to join her sisters and prepare for bed. Julia Smythe Wayne Hartridge was a fascinating and mysterious persona to Emelyn. She got as close to her mother as was allowed. Yet even at a safe distance Emelyn could feel the pain in Julia Hartridge's heart. No matter how beautiful Julia Hartridge looked while entertaining, there was no hiding the sorrow Emelyn saw in her mother's eyes. Emelyn had come to recognize that sorrow each time her mother's eyes glazed over when her father didn't return home as expected. Now that sorrow seemed to be a permanent fixture, hiding the sparkle that once shined in the eyes of Emelyn's mother.

As time went on, Julia Wayne Hartridge took to her room more often. A bottle of laudanum now joined the water, ice, and rag for her head that sat on her bedside table. Julia Hartridge now spent the majority of her time secluded in her room surrounded in the dark calm brought on by the heavy drapes and the dream-like sleepiness of the opiate laudanum.

Julia Smythe Wayne Hartridge died February 1, 1884. Emelyn was twelve years old. Emelyn already had made the commitment to herself that she would not live the life of a socialite. She would have a career outside the home. For now, however, she would dedicate herself to raising her siblings.

Emelyn was still staring out the window, remembering her mother and her own childhood that seemed to be cut too short, when she was brought back to reality by her father's voice: "Emelyn, are you listening to me? Emelyn, I am trying to talk to you!"

Emelyn slowly turned to look at her father. Her face was sullen yet strong. Emelyn was committed to finding strength in adversity, and she would face this situation with the determination to move forward and do her best.

"I understand," Emelyn acknowledged. "I only wish school was not so far from home. I don't want to leave my family. I worry about all of you, especially Katherine."

Emelyn's father moved closer to Emelyn. He leaned over and kissed the top of her head. "You have worried and cared for this family for far too long now, Lyn. It is time now for you to take care of yourself."

Emelyn continued to sit at the edge of her bed. She looked into her father's eyes and forced a smile. She loved it when her father called her Lyn. He had softened. She knew he understood, but she also knew he wasn't going to change his mind. She stood and kissed his cheek.

"I understand," Emelyn reassured her father. "Katherine will be fine living with our aunt and uncle in northern Georgia. It may actually be helpful to her. The past couple of years have been difficult, and the break may do her good. I know I will do well in school and am privileged to be able to go."

Alfred Lamar let out a deep sigh and hugged his daughter tightly.

"Thank you, Lyn. Having your understanding and cooperation makes this so much easier."

He let go of his embrace, patted Emelyn on her head, turned and left the room.

After combing through the many boxes and files, it was clear that as a young girl, Emelyn enjoyed a childhood of relative freedom. She and her siblings spent countless hours playing Blind Man's Bluff, Pick Up Sticks, and Hide and Seek. Their home in Beaulieu allowed Emelyn and her family the luxury to swim, boat and picnic right in their own back yard. But the onset of adolescence signified a time of increased restraint for Emelyn, both in conduct and appearance. Letting down skirts and pulling up one's hair represented a coming of age, and her mother's death did not allow Emelyn additional time to linger in childhood. Ready or not, Emelyn had entered womanhood, a place where carefree play was replaced with self-denial and service to others.

Antebellum woman, such as Emelyn's mother, had been educated in Southern charm and grace. Despite their repressed status, most elite Southern women supported the patriarchal system that had long controlled their lives and were as devoted to the Confederate cause as elite Southern men. Emelyn had watched as her mother's support of such a system not only controlled her life, but took her life.

Emelyn was living in the post-war era, and she strongly believed young women must be educated outside the traditional boundaries of elite womanhood. Women could no longer rely on marriage to provide financial stability. Women needed to learn employable skills, freeing them from relying on monetary support from a husband.

Emelyn was well aware that Southern schools for girls had been geared to teach young women how to be good mistresses, hostesses, and social companions. She knew Vassar boasted a curriculum comparable to that of men's colleges. Although Emelyn knew she was privileged to have a liberal father who encouraged equal education for both his sons and daughters, she didn't feel she had to travel north to New York to receive it. She also did not like that the travel and tuition expenses limited the number of woman who could benefit from such an education. Emelyn made the commitment to go to Vassar. She also made the commitment to herself that after graduation, she would come home and open a prep school right in the city of Savannah. This would allow other young woman to receive a high-quality education without having to leave the security of Savannah and their homes. She would create a school environment where girls felt comfortable and valued while receiving an outstanding college-prep education. Students would be more open to learning if they felt the security of a nurturing home community.

Emelyn learned to hide her pain by wearing a stoic mask and immersing herself in her studies. She learned that if she kept busy with academia, she didn't have time to acknowledge the hurt within her heart.

I instantly connected to Emelyn's passion and need to open a school. Our desires to educate high-school aged youth were born from a desire to heal ourselves.

CHAPTER 20: COINCIDENCE?

This planet is a large school, and our task here is to learn and to grow. —*Dr. Brian Weiss*

Emelyn Hartridge's mother died and her family dynamics forever changed when she was only twelve years old. My parents separated and my family dynamics forever changed when I was only twelve years old. Emelyn Hartridge's father became involved with and married a woman who was young enough to be his daughter. My mother became involved with and married a man old enough to be her father. At fifteen, Emelyn Hartridge was sent away from her home to an out-of-state prep school while her father and new wife created a life together. At fifteen, I was sent out of state to live with my father while my mother and her new husband started a life together. It was her experience of being sent away from home that sparked Emelyn Hartridge's commitment to open a school. It was my experience of being sent away from home that sparked my commitment to open a school.

The similarities were startling. I couldn't help but feel a mutual passion for education that ran much deeper than academics. We wanted to give teenagers a sense of home, a sense of security, a sense of belonging, a sense of accomplishment. We wanted to heal our own hurt by healing others. Learning about Emelyn Hartridge's life helped me to learn about my own. As Oprah would say, another "a-ha" moment. Another piece to the puzzle found and put in place.

But why? Why had Emelyn Hartridge come to me in past life regressions? Why were my memories of her so clear? Had she been sent by divine intervention to change my life? Even if she had not been sent to do so, Emelyn Hartridge was a large part of my life-changing, life-saving journey. If I hadn't attended Dr. Weiss' workshop, would I ever have learned of Emelyn's existence?

I had confirmed a great deal about Emelyn during my January trip to Savannah, but much more would unfold. Unfortunately, Tracey did not have the same experience. Although I felt strongly that perhaps Tracey's regression memories were of Emelyn Hartridge's sister Elizabeth, or "Bessie" as her family had called her, Tracey wasn't convinced. She decided to put her energies elsewhere and pursue classes in holistic healing. Although her decision ended our joint trips to Savannah, my journeys to the city continued.

Escaping the gray skies, cold wind, and snow of February in New Jersey is a gift I couldn't wait to open. Jennifer was safely buckled in the back seat of the car with the bag of snacks and drinks within reach and her American Girl doll safely buckled in the seat beside her. My husband had efficiently placed the last of the suitcases in the trunk, and my oldest son, Michael, was left with his list of marching orders, which consisted of taking care of the Pugs and the house while we were away.

I was on my way back to Savannah. We were taking a family vacation and would be staying in our Hilton Head timeshare. We would be celebrating Jennifer's and my husband's birthdays. I would be taking time to return to Savannah, to the Historical Society, to discovering a former life that remained too close to the present.

The women working in the Historical Society recognized me as I approached the front desk.

"Are you back to do more research on the Hartridge family?" one of the women asked. It felt good to be recognized here. It felt normal.

I sat in the quiet of the Historical Society, savoring every moment of reading letters written during a different century and reliving the life that played out in the corners of my memory. I read numerous letters, documents, and newspaper articles. One article made me gasp. It was the article announcing that Mr. Alfred

Lamar Hartridge was purchasing a Victorian home in Savannah for his daughter Emelyn to open a private school for the girls of the city. Her father supported her. Her father bought her the building that allowed Emelyn to fulfill her mission to provide an upstanding local prep school so the girls of Savannah would not have to leave home. Could this be why I had felt so strongly that my father would provide me the seed money for a school building? Could this be why I had become so emotionally distraught when I learned that I would never get the support I felt I once had from my father?

The other piece to the puzzle was that it was a Victorian home in which Emelyn began her years of owning a school. A Victorian home. The very type of building that I knew I had to have for my school. The very type of building that drove my real estate agent crazy trying to find. The very type of environment I had created as a child playing school in the basement of my home. Is this where my vision came from? Had it been a memory embedded in my soul that I craved to recreate, or was this coincidence?

Coincidence. Definition:

1. The state or fact of occupying the same relative position or area in space.
2. A sequence of events that although accidental seems to have been planned or arranged.

I was beginning to believe that perhaps there was no such thing as coincidence.

I completed my research for the day and jotted down the address where Emelyn's school had been. Chances were that it was no longer there, but I needed to see for myself. It was a beautiful late afternoon in Savannah. The sky was a crystal clear blue, and the sun was still shining brightly. I decided to leave my car parked by the Historical Society and walk to the address on the paper I held tightly in my hand. The Savannah streets were filled with students from the Savannah College of Arts and Design riding to and from their classes and dorms, while the squares were busy with people walking their dogs after a long day at the office. I walked at a brisk pace, still taking time to smile and say hello to the people I passed, but it was clear that I was walking with purpose. I had a mission.

The vibrant colors and decorative gingerbread trim adorning the houses let me know that I was close to the Victorian section of historic Savannah where Emelyn Hartridge pioneered her school. I took out the folded piece of paper that I had tucked into my jacket pocket and read the address. The walk had been an easy one from the Historical Society. As I walked from West Gaston Street towards the address on East Gaston, I watched the large, boxy Greek Revival mansions with their gray brick and stucco exteriors fade behind me, giving birth to complicated, asymmetrical homes with large, wraparound porches, ornamental spindles, imposing roof lines and many gables facing in different directions.

I slowed my pace when the home styles changed and took notice of the street numbers. I knew there was a great chance that the home that housed Emelyn's school no longer existed. I knew there was a chance that numbering of the houses had changed over the years. I also knew I would find it.

Lovely Victorian homes painted in multiple layers are often referred to as Painted Ladies. The home I was looking for was in or near the painted lady section of town.

As I approached the home, I noticed the "for sale" sign posted in the small front property. Alongside the sign was a container holding flyers with details about the house. I quickly grabbed a flyer. I didn't read much because my eyes would not go beyond the sentence I had just read:

"This was once the home to Emelyn Hartridge's school for girls."

Another coincidence?

I took a step back and drank in the stately Victorian home, with the large white front porch. Soon, my feet were moving my body towards the home, up the stairs, and onto the front porch, the one that I saw and desired for my own school building. My trembling hand gently touched the door of the home. Slowly, I allowed my hand to glide across the door and press against the front of the building. It was like sparks going through my body. I could feel an energy rise from my toes to the tip of my head, then I began to shake as chills went down my spine. If I was to believe in past life regression, then I was to believe that I was Emelyn Hartridge in a previous life. If I was to believe that I had been Emelyn Hartridge, then I was to believe that I was standing on the porch of the home that was once my school. If I was to believe that Mr. Hartridge was my father, then I was to believe that I was a daughter my father loved enough to support her dream. What did I believe? I believed that for some reason I was being guided by spirit on a journey of self-discovery.

Chapter 21: Silence of the Cemetery

True intelligence operates silently. Stillness is where creativity and solutions to problems are found. —Eckhart Tolle

After enjoying a leisurely breakfast with my family and spending the morning hours at the pool with Jennifer, I once again traveled from Hilton Head to Savannah to do more research. This afternoon I was not going to the Historical Society. I was going to do my research elsewhere. Today, I was going to explore Bonaventure Cemetery.

Bonaventure Cemetery is east of the Savannah Historic District and rests on a scenic bluff of the Wilmington River. The site of this nearly100-acre cemetery was once a plantation and is the largest of the municipal cemeteries. The land was purchased for a private cemetery in 1846 and became a public cemetery in 1907. With its tree-lined dirt roadways, well-known permanent residents, breathtaking sculptures, and haunting beauty, Bonaventure has been a famous tourist destination for more than 150 years. Another reason behind Bonaventure's popularity is "The Book," Midnight in the Garden of Good and Evil, by John Berendt. The famous "Bird Girl" statue, formerly located in Bonaventure, was featured on the cover of the book, and the movie featured scenes taking place in Bonaventure cemetery. The release of Midnight in the Garden of Good and Evil increased Savannah tourism and Savannah cemetery vandalism, which is one of the reasons Bonaventure now closes at 5 p.m.

Bonaventure cemetery is where Emelyn Battersby Hartridge is buried.

As a child, I found solace spending afternoons reading a book, riding my bike or picnicking in the town cemetery. As an adult, the only time I spent in a cemetery was when I was attending a funeral. I had to admit that I was looking forward to exploring Bonaventure and reconnecting with a pastime of my childhood.

As I rode my bicycle through the cemetery gate, I felt a wave of calm engulf my body. The large, white basket, adorned with multicolored plastic flowers fastened to the handlebars, bounced as my front tire hit a small pothole in the road. I quickly took a hand off the handlebar and covered the top of my bike basket to ensure that the treasures I had so carefully chosen did not fall out. My fast-paced pedaling slowed to a glide as I entered the quiet, rambling cemetery road. The sweet smell of flowers, the warmth of the sun on my face, and the familiar turns in the winding road relieved my twelve-year-old mind and body from the stress brought by raging hormones and the separation of my parents.

I slowly applied the brakes as I approached my favorite spot in the cemetery. I dismounted my bike, put down the kickstand and carefully unloaded the items in my basket. With my arms full, I walked across the grassy knoll until I reached the small pond. I placed the items on the cool marble bench that overlooked the water. From the items, I carefully lifted a small plastic bowl. The bowl was covered with a plastic lid in which I had meticulously punctured several small holes. I took the plastic bowl to the edge of the pond.

The afternoon sun glimmered against the water, causing me to squint as I looked past my reflection and into the murky water of the pond. Soon I could see clearly the many lovely fish swimming towards the top of the water. The majority of the fish were gold, with beautiful white fanning tails. I sat by the edge of the pond and slowly opened the lid that was covering the bowl. Inside, Goldie was swimming happily, even if she didn't have much room to explore in this temporary home.

"I love you, Goldie," I quietly said as I watched her mouth search the top of the water. "You have been a friend to me for years now. I don't know how many kids can say they were lucky enough to have a pet fish live as long as you have. Other goldfish have come and gone, but you are special. You are

a survivor. It is selfish for me to continue to keep you. You have outgrown your bowl, and you must be lonely not having other fish to swim with. I have been coming to this pond for years. The fish here seem nice, and they look like you. They seem happy, and there is plenty of room for you to swim and grow. Please know that I am letting you go because I love you. Things at home are crazy. My father is talking about moving to another state, and I heard mom say she doesn't know if she can afford the house on her own. You deserve a permanent home with other fish that will love you. I promise I will visit you and bring food to feed you. You will be fine. I love you and thank you for being the best goldfish anyone could ever have."

I wiped the tears from my face, picked up the bowl, and slowly poured Goldie into the pond with the rest of the fish. I watched as the other fish approached her, and my eyes followed Goldie and the others as they quickly swam away.

"Be free. Be happy. Be home," I whispered.

I returned to the marble bench and opened the brown paper bag that held my lunch. As I unwrapped the peanut butter and jelly sandwich I had made earlier that morning, I listened carefully to the sounds of silence that enveloped me. The quiet of the cemetery allowed me to enjoy the rustling of the leaves as squirrels chased each other up a tree, the whistling of birds as they spoke in song, the soft splash of the water gently reminding me of my friend's new home, and the sound of my breath filling my lungs, keeping rhythm with my heart. It was silence that allowed me to hear.

It was quiet once again. The familiar feelings of comfort that I experienced during my childhood trips to the cemetery were with me now as I entered the gates of Bonaventure. The grand moss-covered oak trees provided much needed shade from the Savannah sun as I wandered through Bonaventure cemetery in hopes of finding her grave.

I had no map to find Emelyn's grave. I had no reference, no GPS, no directions. What I did have was faith. What I did have was intuition. I closed my eyes and asked the universe to please guide me to my former self and then set my internal compass to "trust." In the quiet of the large cemetery, I listened to my inner voice gently guide me along the dirt roads, directing my body to turn left, right, or continue straight at each crossroad. In what seemed to be no time at all, I found myself standing in the Hartridge family plot where bodies that once housed the souls of Emelyn, her parents, and her sister Ella were laid to rest. I stood staring at the plot, fighting disbelief that an unseen force had guided me here.

"Is this the woman in my past life regression?" I asked out loud to the energy that surrounded me but was not visible to the naked eye.

In the quiet of the moment I heard a resounding "yes" echo throughout my body. A warm breeze touched my cheek, and in the distance I could hear a tour guide sharing the history of the magnificent Bonaventure with a group of people who were eagerly snapping pictures of the breathtaking headstones and pieces of art.

I sighed as I sat on the stone edging of the Hartridges' burial plot. I looked up at the sky and basked my face in the warmth of the sun. Bonaventure was the most beautiful cemetery I had experienced. The dusty lanes shaded by old oak trees covered in Spanish moss, the elaborate Gothic Victorian grave markers, the view of the Wilmington River, and the silent sounds that echo in this city of the dead contribute to Bonaventure's beauty. It is no wonder that this site has captured the attention and imagination of writers, artists, filmmakers, poets, and photographers.

Being in Bonaventure was a spiritual experience. It offered a true reflection of the romanticized and ritualized views of death during the Victorian era. An era in which families were encouraged to spend Sunday afternoons dining in cemeteries with their departed loved ones. Taking the horse and carriage to the park-like setting to meet family and friends for a picnic in the cemetery was the norm during this time period. If I believed I was Emelyn Hartridge in a past life, it would explain why I felt picnicking in a cemetery as a child in this life was a completely normal activity, wouldn't it? The more I let go of my rational thought, the more I allowed myself to explore other explanations for my life experiences.

Emelyn had been determined to create a school for girls in the city of Savannah. She was determined that girls wouldn't have to leave their hometown to receive a proper prep school education.

However, after ten years of fighting political issues and the mindset of the Southern elite, Emelyn left her dream school behind to take a principal position in New Jersey. Emelyn ended up leaving Savannah for the majority of her adult life. Yet, here I sat in Emelyn's final resting place, in the beautiful grounds of Bonaventure, back home in Savannah, the very place she did not want to leave as a fifteen-year-old student. Was it a coincidence that ten years after its inception, I stopped fighting for my school? Was it coincidence that I lived in New Jersey, yet from the first moment I stepped foot in Savannah I knew I was home?

Home. Everyone deserves one. However, I was learning that home does not necessarily mean a large house, manicured lawn, and cable television. *Home: the place or region where something is native or most common.* I was home.

While I was in Bonaventure Cemetery connecting with the past, my husband and daughter had stayed at the Hilton Head resort, enjoying a day of swimming in the pool and collecting shells on the beach. As I drove the fifty-minute commute from Savannah back to Hilton Head, I was deep in thought. I had to admit that I was beyond fascinated with my discoveries. I was beyond intrigued with the messages I had received, the regressions I had experienced, and the facts I had found. There was a lesson to learn, and I was going to learn it. There were messages to receive, and I was going to receive them. There were people who needed to be heard, and I was going to listen. There was a story to tell, and I was going to tell it.

There is more in the environment than what we are able to comprehend with our five senses. There is a sixth sense. It is this sixth sense that allows us entry to another world of vibrational energy, a world of spirit. This sixth sense is intuition, and I was going to use it.

Chapter 22: Life of Service

Your soul mission is your reason for being, your life purpose. It's your calling in life — who you feel called to be, what you feel called to do. Mission is an energy that flows through you — a drive, voice, or passion that you cannot ignore... It's what you know in your heart you must live if you are to experience inner peace and harmony. —Author/Coach Alan Seale

The twelve-hour car ride from Hilton Head back to New Jersey gave me much time for reflection. Time to compare my life with Emelyn Hartridge's. Time to contemplate whether I believed I had found my "past life." Time to examine the similar behaviors, beliefs, and traits that Emelyn and I shared. In our early teens, Emelyn and I experienced family trauma and change. We longed for the security of "home." Emelyn Hartridge and I both created schools with the mission of making students feel at "home." Emelyn Hartridge and I both allowed our schools to become *our* "homes." Emelyn Hartridge and I both lived in New Jersey, but loved and longed for Savannah.

As our car hummed along U.S. 95 North, Jennifer was soundly sleeping in the back seat, while my husband listened to music, carefully navigating around other cars on the highway, and I sat in the passenger seat allowing my mind to recall the letter Emelyn Hartridge had written to her niece. I had held the letter in my hand only days ago, while researching in the Georgia Historical Society. The message was all too familiar.

Emelyn Hartridge received the invitation to her nephew's graduation. How could she possibly attend? She couldn't leave the school. She couldn't leave the students. It was exam week. She was needed. How would the school function without her? How would she function without the school? Emelyn wrote to her sister explaining that it was exam week and she needed to stay at the school to support her girls, her students. Surely you understand, she explained to her sister. I am needed. I am wanted. I matter. I couldn't possibly leave to attend my nephew's graduation. There would be plenty of other family events for Emelyn to attend, but not now. Her girls and her school needed her.

A century later I received the invitation to my cousin's out-of-state wedding. How could I possibly go? I would have to miss the first week of my school's summer program. The students would need me. Who would make sure things ran smoothly? Who would tend to the needs of my students, to the needs of my school? I couldn't possibly make this work. How could the school function without me? How would I function without the school? I will have to decline the invitation. Surely my cousin will understand. I am needed. I am wanted. I matter. There will be other family events to attend, but not now. My students and my school need me.

During my research of Emelyn I came across an original mission statement for her school: Each child is treated as an individual whose work is respected by others and who in turn respects the work of others. As I dug deeper into my research, I discovered more about the philosophies and vision of Emelyn Hartridge's school. Every member of the Hartridge School faculty believes in a personal approach to educating and developing the whole child. Educators take the time, care, and interest in each student to call forth her best work. Integrity is the school's bedrock value. The diversity of thought, background, and culture enriches the school's community. The school community is distinguished by an ethos of care and mutual respect. The Hartridge School provides an educational atmosphere characterized by academic challenge, support for individual excellence, diversity, and a familial sense of community. When faculty members, students, parents, or graduates walk through the doors of the Hartridge School, they have entered a home.

I had lost my breath when I first read the mission statement of the Hartridge School. It was so close to my school's philosophy and mission statement, yet hers had been written a century before mine. I recall how writing my school's mission came so easily. It was something I had known for years:

The school provides a warm, supportive, structured environment in which all students feel welcomed, accepted, and at home. The dignity and worth of each student is recognized and the importance of individual differences and potentialities are celebrated. The school is characterized by its supportive atmosphere and individualized approach that focuses on developing the whole child. The school's objective is to maximize academic success for every student while fostering personal and civic virtues such as integrity, courage, responsibility, honesty, kindness, and respect.

Emelyn Hartridge and I had very similar visions. Clearly we both wanted the students to feel respected and to create a school environment in which the students felt at home. Clearly we both wanted to create for others the things we felt we had needed in our own lives.

A picture of Emelyn Hartridge's school was proudly displayed on the front of the Christmas cards she sent yearly to family and friends. A 1938 newspaper article stated that Emelyn Hartridge's life was devoted to helping others. A 1940 newspaper article stated that Emelyn Hartridge and her Associate Principal, Miss Elizabeth Mapelsden, devoted their entire lives to the school, and it is to them that its success is due. Miss Hartridge and Miss Mapelsden were not only co-workers; they became family. They sincerely loved and cared for their school, their students, and their work. They sincerely loved and cared for each other.

Emelyn Hartridge and Elizabeth Mapelsden both retired on June 30, 1940. After retiring, they spent time traveling together, but they felt lost without their school, their purpose, their life. Elizabeth Mapelsden died July 24, 1941, only a year after retirement.

"Oh, Catherine, how I wish you could have stayed with me longer!" Emelyn wrote to her nephew's wife. *"I don't know how I would have survived if you had not come to stay with me last month."* It was September 1941. Catherine Hartridge, who had married Emelyn's nephew, Walter, had traveled from Savannah to New York City to spend the month of August taking care of Emelyn after the death of Elizabeth. Elizabeth's death left Emelyn overwhelmed with grief. She had lost the person who had been closest to her over the past

thirty-six years. Without her school and without her school family, Emelyn was lost.

Months after Elizabeth Mapelsden's death, Emelyn Hartridge wrote her will and returned to Savannah for a few weeks, rekindling many long lost relationships and connections. She allowed herself to feel at home once again. Emelyn's overdue Savannah visit prompted her to make the decision to start a new life. She wanted to move back to Savannah but would have to live somewhere else during the summer heat. She returned to New York and began to give away her belongings to prepare for new beginnings. Returning to Savannah was the only happiness Emelyn had experienced since the death of her dear friend, Elizabeth.

In a letter dated August 27,1942, Emelyn once again wrote to her cousin-in-law, Catherine Hartridge.

"I am sending you, dear Catherine, my precious Lenox breakfast set and Elizabeth's breakfast tray. Please use this breakfast set and tray for yourself each morning. I have decided to break my promise about never traveling again, and I hope to return to Savannah and start my new life."

Emelyn never made it back to Savannah. On September 24, 1942, she died in her home from heart failure. I believe she may have died of a broken, lonely heart. She was 71 years old. Emelyn had left behind barely enough money to cover her funeral expenses. Everything else she willed to Madolin Mapelsden, a relative of her dear friend Elizabeth. Emelyn lived only two years after her retirement.

After Dr. Weiss' workshop, my drive to research my regression was to find proof to quiet the skeptic inside me. Proof to support an experience that was difficult to explain. Proof that would give me permission to explore a world I believed to be true but suppressed for fear of judgment.

My research brought me to Emelyn, an extraordinarily brave woman who stayed strong in her convictions during an era when that was difficult for a woman who believed in the reform of education, dedicating her life to holistic learning and the care of young minds. The school was her home. The students were her children.

The staff became her family. The end of her career left her sad. The end of Elizabeth left her unwilling to continue living.

Had I been following in Emelyn's footsteps? The school had become my home, where I spent the majority of my weekends and more than sixty hours during the week. The students had become my children, taking more time than I spent with my own daughter. The staff had become my family. I not only spent work time with them, but spent time socializing and planning outside of work. I spent very little time with anyone who was not part of the school.

My intentions were always to support and help struggling students, and yes, I was doing that. But it became unbalanced. It came at a cost of healthy relationships and boundaries. If I continued with the school, would I have lost my family? Would the school be my life? Would I, too, have died once I stopped working? Or would I have died working? Letting go of my school was difficult. But I had not quite alienated myself entirely from other important pieces in my life. I still had my own children to care for, a husband's shoulder to lean on, and the gift of a journey presented to me at Dr. Weiss' workshop. The workshop had swung a door wide open, inviting me to explore something new and unknown while quietly whispering the reassuring message that everything would be okay.

Discovering Emelyn helped me discover behaviors I needed to change within myself. Perhaps I was recreating history and it was time to change course. It felt as though I had received an intervention. Perhaps it was time to embrace a connection to spirit that I had buried, to use this gift to heal and inspire others while healing myself..

I needed to explore whether I could communicate with spirits in the afterlife. I had given a stranger at the workshop a message from spirit that saved her life. Would I be able to do that again for others? I needed to know.

Once we returned to New Jersey I began exploring the world of spiritual mediumship.

Part II: Mediumship

At some point, the illusion breaks down and the opening for the start of the spiritual quest commences. The quest turns from without to within and the search for answers begins. — Psychiatrist and Mystic Dr. David R. Hawkins (1927–2012)

CHAPTER 23: FORGIVING FATHER

We are not human beings on a spiritual journey. We are spiritual beings on a human journey. — Philosopher Pierre Teilhard de Chardin ***(1881-1955)***

Although it was April, a strong, cold wind blew with all its might, prying at the buttons that were struggling to keep my coat closed as I walked the typical brisk pace of a New Yorker fighting the crowds to reach her destination.

James Van Praagh, a psychic medium, was in New York City, teaching, lecturing and displaying his skills of mediumship. I had found this out once we returned from Hilton Head. I quickly signed up for the three-day course and went to the library to read all of his books.

As I walked into the Manhattan hotel where the workshop was held, I was struck by how far my journey had taken me. It was hard to believe that a year ago I had been in Philadelphia attending Dr. Brian Weiss' workshop, and now I was going to learn from a respected medium.

I took a seat in one of the many rows of chairs facing a platform stage in the large banquet room. I watched as people flowed in, some holding books in anticipation of receiving autographs from the many well-known spiritual authors who had gathered to share their personal growth stories.

The Omega Institute for Holistic Studies was hosting the event. Omega was founded on the holistic worldview that the wellbeing of each of us is deeply connected to the wellbeing of all living things. The institute offers educational experiences geared to inspire personal change. This conference offered workshops and lectures by about sixteen authors offering unique tools for living a more authentic life. They included Geneen Roth, the *New York Times* best-selling author of Women, Food and God. Roth gave a keynote address on the relationship between food, money, and what is enough. She openly discussed the lessons she learned following the loss of her entire life-savings in the Bernie Madoff scandal. Other authors included Elizabeth Lesser, Byron Kathleen, and, of course, James Van Praagh. Conference participants could choose from several in-depth workshops on themes such as meditation skills, breaking through fear, the meaning of happiness, connecting to the world of spirit, balancing energy, and more.

Van Praagh's workshop description said participants would learn how to release old soul patterns of negative behavior, retrieve past life memories and experiences for the soul's optimal growth and integrate the emotional, spiritual, physical, and mental selves. Students would understand the mechanics of mediumship and receive messages from the spiritual realm to enhance our lives and connection to the world of spirit. We would also learn how to demonstrate and read spirit messages and psychic insights in front of a group, as well as develop an awareness of intuition, balance, harmony, and healing through visual imagery, mediations, mind journeys, and insightful dialogue. I couldn't wait. I sat in the front row and held my breath with anticipation for the next phase of my journey.

Van Praagh's easygoing manner, sense of humor, and his ability to laugh at himself relaxed me. He displayed his mediumistic talents by performing several group readings, which did not leave much of an impression with me. It wasn't until we began our meditations using visual imagery that my interest was truly captured.

Van Praagh dimmed the lights. Using a CD player, he began playing beautiful and emotional music. He instructed us to connect with our breath and close our eyes. We were to attach to mother earth and visualize our bodies filled with a green light of love, joining our feet to the earth as if we were rooted to the ground. He asked us to picture a door. We were to open the door and walk through it to a warm glowing light. In the light were our departed loved ones. We were to picture them sitting at a banquet table and join them. We were to spend time with them and ask them for messages. Van Praagh took me on a journey in my mind to another world, where I felt my departed loved ones with me.

I could see both sets of grandparents sitting at the table. My mother's father who physically assaulted me before putting me on the train was there with my grandmother, the woman he had divorced, the woman I bonded with as she was dying in the care of hospice. On the other side of the banquet table were my father's parents. My loving grandmother who secretly fought the demons within by drowning her feelings with alcohol was sitting next to my grandfather whose death when I was five years old had prompted my father's tears. I looked longingly at the table. I noticed how beautiful my grandparents looked. I felt surrounded in a wave of love and forgiveness. Tears were flowing down my face, not only in my visualization, but down the face of the body that was sitting in this workshop. I noticed an empty spot. My father was missing from this banquet table.

At the head of the table was a seat that looked like a small throne. It was gold and upholstered in red velvet. My grandparents instructed me to sit in this chair. It felt uncomfortable to be at the head of the table in a seat of honor. I did as I was told. Where was he? I guess I should not have been surprised that my father once again did not show up. He once again was absent from my life.

My father's mom stood up from the table and gave me a kiss on the cheek. She walked to the other side of the room where a curtain hung against the wall. She slowly opened the veil, and my father stepped forward. My grandparents stood as my father approached me while I sat awestruck in my throne. My tears were no longer silent. They were audible, and I felt the woman next to me slip a tissue into my hand.

My father held out his hand to me, and I reached forward, allowing our hands to clasp. Holding my hand, my father slowly walked me to the center of the room as my grandparents stood watching. I could hear the music. Was it the music in my mind or the music Van Praagh was playing? In my father's embrace, we began to dance. It was the closest I had ever been to him.

"I am so very sorry," my fathered whispered as I rested my head on his chest and followed his lead on the dance floor. "I was a troubled man. I didn't know how to love you the way you needed to be loved. I didn't know how to be a father. But I did love you, and I am proud of you. You are beautiful. You are enough. Please forgive me."

I lifted my head and allowed our eyes to meet. "I do forgive you. I do! I understand. Thank you. Thank you."

I allowed my eyes to wander around the room and saw that my grandparents were smiling. Tears of love glimmered in their eyes. I turned back to look at my father. He gave me a hug. As he disengaged from our embrace he kept his eyes locked on mine and began walking backwards, toward the curtain, and he was once again gone. I looked at my grandparents who were still smiling in my direction and watched as one by one they disappeared from sight.

I heard Van Praagh's voice gently bringing us home from this altered state and returning my mind to the physical world. I opened my eyes to find that I was soaked with tears.

The woman next to me squeezed my hand.

"You must have had a very emotional reunion with your loved ones," she whispered.

I did. It was surreal. I felt as though I had actually been with my father. It was a healing experience. It was what I needed.

After this exercise, we had a lunch break. I quickly went to the woman's bathroom, wet a paper towel, and washed my tear-streaked face. Although the image in the mirror looked a mess, I never felt more beautiful. There was a glow that had not been there before. It was the glow of forgiveness. It was the glow of love.

After lunch we returned to the workshop to engage in activities to develop our psychic and medium abilities. As in Dr. Weiss' workshop, we were paired with a stranger. Our partner had to give us the first name of someone who had passed, and we were to concentrate and share any images or thoughts that came to us.

I sat facing my partner. Her skin wrinkled around the corners of her hazel eyes as her warm smile welcomed me.

"I am excited to do this," she staid while nervously tucking her ash brown hair behind her ears, revealing several streaks of gray near her temples.

"I am, too!" I replied. "Have you chosen a name yet?"

Without hesitation, my partner announced the name Sally. I gave my partner my father's name, Burt. Van Praagh instructed us to sit quietly in a meditative state allowing images and thoughts to come to us, until he announced it was time to share our findings.

My partner shared first. "I kept seeing images of a dog," she said. "I believe that Burt is a dog that you lost. You and Burt were very close."

The expression on my face must have clued my partner that her message was inaccurate. My partner went on to explain that she thought I had given her a fake name. I had to laugh.

After my partner had given me the name Sally, I gently closed my eyes and almost immediately a woman in her mid-forties, with a wide smile, appeared to me. She showed herself in a hospital bed and made me feel as though she had suffered for quite some time. She ran her fingers through her hair, gently tossing her curls. The warm tingle that ran through my body was an indication to me of how much this woman loved and appreciated my partner. I saw my partner standing next to the hospital bed, holding the woman's hand. The woman did not seem conscious, but her soul knew that my partner was with her. My partner appeared in this vision the way she looked now. I knew this death was recent.

Now it was my turn to share.

"Sally comes across to me as a very close friend. In fact, she makes me feel as though you were more like sisters." As I said these words, my partner's eyes widened as she leaned forward in her chair, positioning herself closer to me.

"Sally's smile would light up a room. Please know she is once again smiling. She wants you to know that she is out of pain and is proudly tossing around her new hair. Sally died fairly recently, and she is letting me know that she suffered a long time with cancer. She was a fighter. She also tells me that you were by her side throughout it all. You put your life on hold for her. You were with her until the end. You gave her the permission and support she needed to move on. She is extremely thankful and loves you very much. She says you have her picture with you."

My partner's tears made her cheeks look ruddy against her alabaster skin. She used the backs of her slender hands to wipe them away, leaving behind faint streaks of memories that leaked from her eyes.

"How do you know this?" she said. "Are you a professional medium?"

"No," I said. "I'm on a journey of self-discovery."

My partner stood, her tall, lanky body hidden under a large pullover sweater. I watched as her long fingers reached into the pocket of her jeans and pulled out a piece of paper. When she handed it to me, I realized it was a picture. I looked at it and saw the same smile that greeted me in the vision. Without being told, I knew it was Sally.

"I came here praying that James Van Praagh would choose me for a reading and that I would hear from Sally, but you just answered all my questions and more. She was my best friend. We were like sisters. I needed to hear that she knew I was with her to the end. I couldn't have received a more accurate and healing message. I no longer need to be at this workshop. Thank you!"

My partner and I embraced. I didn't know what to say. It was a lot to digest. We made eye contact as we said our goodbyes. I noticed a glow to her face that was not there at the start of the exercise. I recognized the glow. I had seen it in the reflection of the bathroom mirror earlier that morning. I watched as she left the workshop. She appeared to be floating as if escorted by an angel.

I once again had shared an intimate moment with someone I did not know. I was connecting with something that could not be seen by the naked eye. I was connecting with the soul.

I was taking steps in a direction that was changing my life – and might change other lives, as well. I left the James Van Praagh workshop with direction.

Chapter 24: Back to School

When the pupil is ready, the teacher will appear. — Unknown

After my New York City workshop with James Van Praagh, I was committed to learn all I could about the world of spirituality and mediumship. I wanted to learn from the best and began researching the experts in the field. I discovered The Arthur Findlay College in England where students can study Spiritualism, healing, the art of mediumship, spiritual and psychic unfolding, and other connected disciplines. I was amazed. I was curious. I was broke.

Although the school was reasonably priced for a private college, I was in no position to pay the tuition, let alone the airfare and travel expense to Great Britain. I was astounded and interested in the variety of courses, levels, and instructors at the college. My desire to learn, but also to save money, led me on a search to find spiritual medium classes offered in the United States. Surprisingly, my search led me to my own back yard: Pompton Lakes, New Jersey.

I came across a website for Janet Nohavec, a Catholic nun who left the convent after discovering her abilities as a medium. She studied for years at the Arthur Findlay College in England and operated the Journey Within Spiritualist Church in Pompton Lakes. In addition to holding services, the church offered appointments for medium and psychic readings, healing, and classes in the art of mediumship. I went to the Journey Within's website and eagerly clicked on *the school of mediumship* tab. I couldn't believe what I discovered. Tutors from the Arthur Findlay College came to the

Journey Within to teach classes right here in good old New Jersey. A class was scheduled for June. Coincidence or was the universe setting this up for me?

Colin Bates is a tutor and course organizer at the Arthur Findlay College, Stansted, England and a tutor and demonstrator at the Spiritualist Association of Great Britain, Belgrave Square in London. He is a registered Spiritualist healer and a public demonstrator of mediumship. He was coming to Pompton Lakes to teach a course in mediumship. He was going to have me as a student. He was going to help open my eyes, my mind, and my heart.

Bates' course was designed to help students become the best possible instrument of spirit. I felt strongly that spirit had been guiding me through my past life regressions and my delivery of accurate messages to two strangers. If I was going to continue my spiritual journey, I wanted to be the best messenger I could be.

Like a giddy schoolgirl beginning a new academic year, I spent the evening before my class choosing my clothes and making sure I had a notebook and pens. I was too nervous to sleep well and spent most of the night tossing and turning, watching the alarm clock, in fear I might oversleep and be late for my first day of school.

I woke early the next morning feeling energized despite little sleep. Butterflies were swirling in my stomach, making it difficult to finish my coffee, and nervous anxiety took away any desire for breakfast, so I decided to just jump in the car and get a head start on my travels. The extra time would allow for any out-of-the-way routes my GPS might have planned for me. I knew that after today, I would be able to get to and from class following my own direction.

I reached my destination with only ten minutes to spare. I took a deep breath as I opened the door to the large room where the class was being held. Chairs were placed in a circle, and I joined the others who were waiting for class to begin. I silently surveyed the room. The raised platform in the front was home to a beautiful wooden podium and four large, throne-like chairs, similar to the one I saw myself sitting in during the meditation with James Van Praagh. The walls and carpet were accented with soft, pastel colors of blues and mauves, and lovely white angels were placed in every corner. I had entered a sanctuary.

Colin Bates had a warm smile and intriguing accent that captivated me from the start. We began class with brief introductions. Many of the students had studied at the Arthur Findlay College, and a few had taken previous classes with Colin. Some students were practicing mediums while others, like me, were new to the journey.

Colin's class was intense. It focused on concentration and meditation through the use of sound and color visualization techniques. Colin explained the energy of the auric field. He taught me how to use my own intuition when interpreting the physical, mental, emotional, and spiritual aspects through color, learning how the color location and clarity of the energy can relay information relating to the physical.

Colin gave an in-depth look at the philosophy of Spiritualism. He helped me to understand mediumship. He taught techniques designed to strengthen and improve communication with the world of spirit and explained clairsentience, clairvoyance, and clairaudience — clear feeling, clear vision, and clear hearing. Most mediums have one or two of these senses that they use to communicate with the spirit world. From my experience, I knew I had all three.

Colin taught the class how to connect and hold a link to the spirit world and how to interpret symbols. I learned how to present the information I received and then had to do so in front of the class. I learned about private medium sittings and how to give meaningful and respectful readings. I drank in all the information with an unquenchable thirst. I was able to give accurate readings to my fellow classmates in both private and public demonstrations.

It was an exhilarating and exhausting experience. Colin worked us the entire time. He had us actively engaged and accepted nothing but our best. At the end of the classes, Colin approached me.

"Please promise me that you will continue to work on your mediumship," he said. "You have a gift, and I expect to see you again."

I was speechless. I was determined. I realized I needed to accept this gift and move forward to the best of my ability.

Chapter 25: Afraid to 'Come Out'

Experience is stronger than belief. What you were taught when you were a young child might be true or not. When you experience, then you know. — Unknown

A year had passed since I concluded that I no longer wanted to be *That Person.* A year without my school, without a career, without a steady income, without missing my daughter's activities, without the stress of constantly doing. A year of being class mom, of greeting my daughter when she returned home from school, of finding pleasure in cooking for my family, walking the dogs, and enjoying the smell of clean sheets on the bed. It had been a year of adventure in an unknown territory. A year of becoming reacquainted with Savannah, Georgia, rediscovering Emelyn and her family, reconnecting with the spiritual world. It had been a year of reflection, slowing down, facing and letting go of old wounds. A year of healing, learning, making soul connections. A year of trusting my intuition.

I had come to accept what I had known as a child. We are surrounded by a world of spiritual energy. There is more in the environment than what we are able to comprehend with our five senses. There is a sixth sense that allows us entry to another world of vibrational energy. This sixth sense is intuition.

Intuition becomes blocked when we allow ourselves to become so busy and consumed with the material world that we no longer take the time to quiet our minds and listen to our inner voice, our higher self. Dr. Weiss' workshop helped guide me to exercise my intuition back into shape, and I had been working hard at it.

I took Reiki classes and became a certified Reiki Master. I took psychic counseling courses with Carol Carbone and became a certified intuitive counselor. I continued taking courses in mediumship at the Journey Within and was privileged to attend classes, workshops, demonstrations, and lectures with Arthur Findlay College instructors Brian Robertson, Simon James, Stella Upton, and Janet Nohavec. I took healing classes and became a certified healer.

I attended weekend workshops in Gettysburg, Pennsylvania, with historian Mark Nesbitt and psychic medium Laine Crosby. They introduced me to tools of the trade such as dowsing rods, pendulums and Electronic Voice Phenomena (EVP), the capturing of spirit voices on a recorder. I participated in investigations of the Cashtown Inn, The Danielle Lady Farm, The Gettysburg Scenic Engine House located on the battlefields, and the Ghosts of Gettysburg Headquarters owned by Mark Nesbitt.

The spiritual energy in Gettysburg was overwhelming. I could feel it. I could see it. I could hear it. It was in Gettysburg that I opened myself to listening to the stories of the soul. I realized once you lift the veil, you open yourself to the invisible world of spirit. I found myself standing between the physical world and the world of spirit, and, like a bridge, I was able to connect the two. I had opened my consciousness through the sixth sense, the intuitive mind.

However, even with all these classes and certifications, I still was not ready to go public with my gift. I was still afraid of what people would think.

The negative inner voice inside me would begin its chatter at the mere thought of sharing my gift outside of the workshop or classroom setting. "People will think you are crazy. All those years of college and earned degrees and THIS is what you are doing? With the exception of your husband, no one else in your family will accept or understand this. This is not practical. This is irresponsible.

This may be what you want to do with your life, but it is not what you SHOULD do with your life."

Living in the world of should is a stressful place to reside. *Should. Have to. Expect. Obliged.* The problem was that I was trying to live up to what I thought were others' expectations of me. Why did I care what others would think? Was a part of me still seeking approval? Was my inner child still fearful of being unloved and alone? Did the fear of rejection surface when I considered doing something that might be seen as unconventional? To resolve this internal conflict, I needed to be authentic and own who I am. I needed to live a fearless life. But how? Where would I find the courage to take the leap of faith, trusting that I would fly?

Entering year two of "unemployment" was easier than year one. I was not longing to go back to traditional work. I had accepted that I no longer wanted a career in the public school system. I was enjoying being home. I had learned to slow down. I had learned to quiet my mind. I had rediscovered pleasure in the simpler things. I had experienced the world of spirit. I had accepted my gift. However, I still was afraid to "come out."

Chapter 26: Leap of Faith

To live, to TRULY live, we must be willing to RISK. To be nothing in order to find everything. To leap before we look. — Mandy Hale, The Single Woman: Life, Love, and a Dash of Sass

It was a stormy day during the end of October. I was alone in the house, sitting quietly on the floor in the family room, with candles lit. The sound of the rain hitting the roof and the darkness of the sky helped me fall into a deep meditation. I soon felt a chill down my spine, and with my eyes closed he appeared, wearing a blue and red checkered flannel shirt and a warm smile. His hair was dark, a bit on the long side. His eyes were gentle, and his face was the beautiful one I remembered. I hadn't seen him since I was a freshman in high school.

Bobby had died tragically at the age of fourteen. He was the younger brother of a girl with whom I attended grade school. Bobby had gone hunting with some friends. One of the friends accidentally shot Bobby in the face, killing him instantly.

I hadn't thought of Bobby in many years. Why had he come to see me today? His presence was strong and urgent. Bobby brought forward his mother. She was with him in the spirit world and had her arm around him. There was a bright white light surrounding them, and I could feel their love. They were happy together.

I watched as his mother rubbed her legs and then twirled, indicating to me that her cause of death had something to do with complications involving her legs, but now she was well. Bobby pleaded, "Please tell my sister, Patti, that we are fine. Please tell her that

Mom's legs have healed. She needed to be with me. She will be a better mother to you now. Please forgive her." Bobby acknowledged his pride in Patti and thanked her for her strength. She had done her best to be the caregiver to her younger siblings. He expressed concern for Patti's oldest son and let me know that he had been there supporting her and her son through a difficult time. Bobby shared other important personal information that he wanted me to relay to Patti.

"I would like to share your message with Patti. I really would," I said. "However, I haven't been in contact with her in more than thirty years. I have no way of knowing how to get in touch with her."

"She will be at your high school reunion next month. Go. You will see her there," Bobby said.

Why would Patti be at my high school reunion? She didn't go to high school with me. She moved out of town our freshman year.

"Trust me," Bobby said. "She will be there. Just go. Tell her what I have said."

I watched as Bobby and his mother faded away. I opened my eyes. What should I do? I had wanted to go to the reunion next month but had some reservations. It was much easier for me to attend these functions when I was able to tell people what I did for a living. I had not yet come up with an acceptable answer to this question, and I knew I would be asked numerous times. After my visit from Bobby, I knew in my gut, my heart, my soul I should go. If Patti was not at the reunion, then I would know I had been hallucinating and perhaps it was time to get a job. But what if Patti was there?

The evening of the reunion I was as nervous as a girl going to her first dance. The night was not just about reconnecting with friends and classmates. It was a test of my abilities, my faith, and the world of spirit.

I drove into the parking lot of the hotel where I was meeting two of my good friends from high school. I pulled up to the hotel entrance where Mary and Traci were waiting. I threw the car in park, jumped out the driver's side door and threw my arms around these gorgeous women.

"You both look amazing!" I squealed. Traci maintained the flawless baby face she had in school, and Mary's body was in stellar shape. We chatted nonstop as I drove to the reunion, which was being held in a restaurant close to the hotel where Traci was staying. I did not mention Patti or my visit from Bobby.

I was skittish. What if Patti was at the reunion? How can I tell someone that I haven't seen in more than thirty years that her deceased brother came and spoke to me? How can I tell her I saw her mother with him? What if her mother has not passed and I tell her this? What if she doesn't remember me? What if she doesn't want to hear what I have to say? What if... What if... What if it is true? What if it is a message she needs to hear in order to heal? I have to trust.

We joined the reunion. Mary was on the planning committee and was pulled away to take care of some last-minute loose ends. Traci and I immersed into the sea of people, looking for familiar faces.

It wasn't long before I saw her. Patti was standing in the middle of the crowded floor, looking lovely, and chatting with other attendees. I ran into the bathroom to catch my breath. Why was she here? After all these years, I recognized her as if it was only yesterday. I stared at my reflection in the bathroom mirror. My shaking hands rummaged through my purse in search of lipstick. While applying the color to my lips I kept reassuring myself to trust my instincts. I left the bathroom, went straight to the bar and ordered a glass of red wine that I finished too quickly.

"Live a fearless life. Move out of your comfort zone. This is a turning point. Trust."

I put the empty long-stemmed wine glass on the bar and walked to the table where Patti was standing with Nancy, a classmate that I knew and had asked to attend the reunion. Nancy and I hugged.

"Do you remember Patti?" Nancy said. "I was very surprised to see her here! It's been so long!"

Nancy hugged us both, and Patti gave me a big hug. "Of course I remember you!" she said.

"I remember you, too!" I said. "We spent many years together in grade school, and I'll never forget the fifth grade end-of-the-year pool party you had at your house! Even Mrs. Brook, our teacher, came to that party! We were all in the pool, singing "Jeremiah Was a Bullfrog" at the top of our lungs. It was a great time and a great memory!"

Patti said, "We did have some good times growing up. Unfortunately I had to move out of town and live with my father once we entered high school. It's funny. I had no intention of attending this reunion. Actually, the high school where I graduated is having their reunion tonight, and I was planning on going there. While grocery shopping last week, I ran into someone from the old neighborhood who told me about this reunion, and I got a strong feeling that this is where I needed to be! So here I am, and I am so happy to be reconnecting with the people who grew up with me. I feel as though I never left!"

Quick. Get me another drink.

Here it was. My opportunity to take the leap of faith or leave myself hanging.

"Patti, you may think I'm crazy," I said. No stopping now. "But do you believe in psychics or mediums?"

"Well, yes. I actually do. I've been to several but haven't gotten the answers I needed. Yet, I do believe. Why?"

"Your brother, Bobby, came to me last month with a message. I'll only share it if you want to hear it. I totally understand if you walk away from me."

"Are you kidding?" Patti said with a gasp as she grabbed my arm with excitement. "I've been going to psychics and mediums in search of a message from my brother and haven't had much luck. I've been waiting for this moment! Please tell me what he said. I would love to hear what you have to share. Please. Don't hold back.'

And with that I shared Bobby's message. I shared personal details. I described the clothes Bobby was wearing and how he appeared to me. Patti was astonished. I had just described what he was wearing and how he looked in a picture she treasured. I told her about her mother and her legs. Patti was shocked. Yes, her mother had passed, and yes, she had blood clots in her legs, which was the cause of her death, but no one knew about this. How did I know? Bobby told me. Patti confirmed Bobby's reason for concern about her oldest son and was relieved to know that Bobby was watching over him. I explained to Patti how Bobby reassured me that she would be at the reunion, giving me the opportunity to share his message, here, with her, tonight.

Patti was crying. She was hugging me.

"You have no idea how I needed to hear what you've told me. I needed to hear that my mother was with Bobby. After he passed, that was all she wanted. I can't thank you enough. What a gift you have. Is this what you do for a living?" she asked.

Ah, there it was, the question.

I took the leap of faith, and I flew. I broke out of my comfort zone. I had received and shared a message that would help a person on her road to healing. There is much more to this than receiving messages. It's the ability to bridge the spiritual and the physical world, with the intention of healing both worlds.

In the moment of this evening, I had followed through with what my inner guidance was telling me. Attachment is guided by ego, and letting go is guided by spirit. To fulfill my higher life purpose, I needed to continue to let go and follow my inner guidance.

Was this what I did for a living? No. But, after the reunion, not only had I reconnected with Patti, I was now confident enough to consider that the path I was on could be leading me to a new career.

Chapter 27: No Coincidence

The real voyage of discovery consists not in seeking new landscapes, but in having new eyes. —Author Marcel Proust (1871–1922)

Patti and I stayed in contact after the reunion. We lived less than an hour away from each other and did our best to see each other regularly. She became one of my biggest cheerleaders and supporters of my gift. She introduced me to others who wanted readings, and I honed my skills by giving free readings. Her support and approval helped me to be open. The more I allowed myself to be open, the more spirit shared with me. I began to receive messages regularly through my meditation. I began to trust in spirit that my messages were accurate, and spirit trusted in me to relay the messages.

He came to me pacing. I had seen him less than a year ago at the class reunion. Before the reunion, I had not seen him in more than twenty years. I had never met his wife. We were not in contact after high school. However, we did connect and speak with each other at the reunion, bantering about our opposing political beliefs and sharing our views on the recent changes in education.

Now, here he was, an old classmate I'll call Tom, frantically pacing, asking me to reach out to his family. Only months after the reunion he had been killed in an accident. His energy was strong and urgent. He was worried about his father, his wife and his children. He had messages to share. He wanted a sit-down meeting with his family. He wanted me to be the bridge to bring the physical and spiritual world together.

But how? I didn't know his wife. His family didn't know me. Once again, I questioned how to handle this. I didn't want to intrude. I prayed for an answer.

The weekend after Tom appeared to me, Patti and I had dinner with a few friends we had reconnected with at the reunion. Someone brought up Tom and how distraught his family had been since his death.

Patti nudged me.

"Say something. Tell them what you can do. Maybe you can help!"

I looked at her as if she had just asked me to pull a million dollars out of my pocket, not able to respond.

Patti could no longer stand my silence. "Diane is a medium," she announced. The table became quiet. "Believe me when I tell you, she is good. She told me things no one knew."

The girls began to talk and ask questions all at once. "Why didn't you tell us?" "That's incredible!" "How did you know?" "How old were you when you suspected you may have the gift?" "I love mediums!" "I watch Long Island Medium every week!" "I go down to the shore every year to see a medium!"

Here was a group of women in their forties excited that I was a medium. They were business owners, nurses, teachers, wives, and mothers supporting my gift. The response was the opposite of what I been playing in my head all these months.

Then someone asked, "Has Tom ever come to you?"

Gulp. I turned off the negative chatter in my head, took a deep breath, and told everyone at the table how Tom came to me and wanted to talk with his family. Without hesitation, Anne, the woman sitting next to me, said she knew the family and felt they needed to hear what I had to say. She explained that Tom's cousin was coming to her house the next day to give her an estimate on some work on her kitchen. She was going to let him know.

The next evening my phone rang. It was Tom's brother. "My cousin told me that Tom came to you. He said that Tom wants a family meeting. I know this is my brother coming through because he was always calling family meetings, and I knew in my heart he would do it again. When can we meet?"

I arrived at Tom's family home the next Tuesday at 7 p.m. The late fall air was cool and damp. It was the time of the year when fall had come to an end yet winter was not yet officially here. It was about six months since Tom's passing and almost a year since the reunion. I walked to the front door of Tom's parents' ranch home where Tom grew up and was greeted warmly by one of his seven sisters. She brought me into the dining room where Tom's parents, sisters, brother, wife, children, and other family members were gathered around the extra large table. There were about twenty people. Surprisingly, I was not nervous. I felt confident. I knew in my heart this was right.

I took a seat at the dining room table where I was surrounded by eyes longing for healing, longing for their loved one. I thanked the family for the privilege of meeting with them and allowing me to share Tom's message. I closed my eyes, opened my internal link to the spirit world and without hesitation Tom stepped forward. He had messages for his family members that made them laugh, cry and connect. The family took turns asking questions. His daughters asked for college advice. His brother asked for confirmation on business decisions. His father asked for validation that it was actually him. Tom did not fail to answer. We shared for hours. It was love. It was a step towards healing.

While I was sharing messages with Tom's family, another male spirit kept trying to get my attention. Like Tom, this male energy was strong and urgent. I let him know that he needed to wait until I was finished, and I would open up to him while I was driving home.

As soon as I started my car and pulled away from Tom's home, I was met with the male energy that had tried to interrupt me earlier. This male came across as anxious. He explained that he was very worried about his wife. He had recently been killed in a car accident. He and his wife were separated at the time. He showed me details of his life with his wife and son. He showed me his car accident and why he felt responsible. He showed me his wife's pain, sorrow, and self-destruction. "Please help her," he pleaded. "She needs you."

"But how?" I gently asked. "I don't know you. I don't know your wife." With that, he appeared with a large disco ball over his head. "I am the disco man," he said. "The first person you talk to tomorrow will know who I am. Tell that person you spoke to the disco man. You will then find my wife."

Chapter 28: The Disco Man

The spiritual journey is individual, highly personal. It can't be organized or regulated. It isn't true that everyone should follow one path. Listen to your own truth. — Ram Dass

The next morning, after getting Jennifer off to school, I poured myself a cup of coffee and sat on the sofa in the family room. I was reflecting on my evening with Tom's family and my conversation with the unknown disco man on my way home. My thoughts were interrupted by the sound of the phone ringing.

I answered and immediately recognized the energetic voice on the other end. It was Patti.

"I couldn't wait any longer to hear how things went last night with Tom's family," Patti said. "I know you won't share private information, but I just want to know if everything went well. I'm sure you were able to give the family some sense of peace."

"Everything went well last night, but something strange happened," I said. "There was a male spirit who interrupted me at Tom's, and then he talked to me almost the whole ride home!"

"Who was it?" Patti said.

"He said he was the disco man and that he was recently killed in a car accident."

"Are you kidding?" Patti said, gasping. "I know who that is! He ran disco events that my husband and I went to. In fact, we had tickets to one of his events for the weekend after he died. His wife lives in the town next to mine. I've been worried about her and have heard she's not doing well. I had been thinking of telling you about her to see if you felt you could help. I can't believe this! I have to call his wife! I'll call you back!"

Before I could reply, Patti had hung up.

Less than an hour later, she called back.

"I spoke to his wife," she said. "I'm bringing you to her house this Sunday!"

As it turned out, the disco man – I'll call him Mike — owned a company that held disco parties in restaurants and other public places. Patti was the first person I had spoken to this morning. She also knew the disco man and was able to connect me with his wife, just as Mike's spirit had told me.

Early Sunday afternoon, I took the fifty-minute ride to Patti's house, which was busy with the comings and goings of her younger son, his friends, and her adult stepchildren who visited on the weekends. Her husband, Carlos, was enjoying his day, watching sports on TV while Patti was busy in the kitchen preparing food and putting it on the table for her family and anyone else who happened to stop by. Everyone always felt welcomed and would never leave hungry from Patti's home.

She kissed me on the cheek as she placed a plate of pepperoni and cheese on the counter. We said our goodbyes to her family as Patti grabbed her coat and purse. Patti was always active, which contributed to her slender build. She and Carlos owned a business specializing in adaptive seating and home health care equipment. Between running her business and caring for her family, Patti was in perpetual motion.

I sat in the passenger seat of her car and thought about how far I had come this past year with accepting and sharing the messages I received. If anyone had told me two years ago that I would be going to the home of a woman I had never met, to share a message I received from her deceased husband, whom I also had never met, I would have thought they were crazy.

Patti and I walked to the front door of the house where Mike's wife – I'll call her Jean – lived, and I immediately noticed the beautiful angel statues in her yard and on the porch. Patti rang the doorbell, and soon a woman with wavy blond hair and sad blue eyes opened the door to greet us. I followed Patti into the house, where she introduced me to Jean.

"Thank you so much for coming here!" Jean said as she brought us into the kitchen and offered us something to drink.

"No, thanks," Patti said. "I'm going to leave you two alone and run a few errands. I'll come back when you're finished."

"I've two chairs set up in my bedroom for us. I thought that might be a quiet, private place to talk," Jean said as I followed her up the stairs to her room.

Her bedroom was filled with candles and angel statues. "Do you mind if I record this?" Jean asked as she motioned to me to sit in one of the chairs.

"Of course not," I replied.

Jean grabbed a piece of paper from her nightstand and took the seat across from me. Her long eyelashes were mascaraed, her nails perfectly manicured and her lips glimmered with sparkling gloss. Yet nothing could mask the redness of her eyes and the tracks of her tears.

Jean's trembling hand clutched the piece of paper she held in front of her.

"I have so many questions to ask, I needed to write them down so I wouldn't forget," she said.

"Let's put the questions aside for now," I said gently. "I'll tell you everything your husband shared with me, and after I tell you everything, then you can ask your questions."

Grounding myself, I placed both feet flat on the carpeted floor. I closed my eyes, breathing deeply, while I made my connection with the world of spirit. Without hesitation, Mike came through, reiterating the things he had told me while driving home from Tom's family. Mike had apologies, regrets, and explanations for things that had transpired in their relationship. He shared facts about his accident that were in the police report, which Jean had not had the strength yet to read. The report confirmed what Mike had disclosed during the reading. What seemed to be only a half an hour ended up to be more than two hours of sharing. Jean looked at her list of questions. When she lifted her eyes from the paper, an expression of astonishment showed on her face.

"Not only did you answer every single question on this list, without me asking, you answered them in order!" Jean said in shock. Mike must have been aware of the list and came through prepared with answers.

When it was time for me to leave, I hugged Jean goodbye. She looked at me with tears falling down her cheeks.

"I felt Mike when I hugged you," she whispered. "I actually felt him."

Meeting with Jean had been an emotional and fulfilling afternoon. The messages and answers came from Mike at a time when Jean needed them most. Jean had wanted to end her life. Mike came through, giving her the information she needed to take a step forward in her healing.

Jean soon spread the word to others about her reading and how I found her. She began inviting people to her home to receive medium readings from me. Many of the people I read in Jean's home invited me to their homes to give readings to their family members and friends. By word of mouth and Patti's and Jean's endorsements, I soon had a waiting list of people wanting to hear healing, evidential words of love from the world of spirit. Spirit had led me to a new calling.

Chapter 29: Evidence from the Other Side

The real test of a man is not how well he plays the role he has invented for himself, but how well he plays the role that destiny assigned to him. — Philosopher Jan Patočka (1907–1977)

I met them at the address they had given me. I pulled the car in the driveway and lowered the driver's side window.

"Park over there," Jason directed as he pointed to a space behind a blue Honda. "We're taking two cars. You can drive with me and Kerry."

I obediently followed Jason to his car and climbed in the back seat. Kerry jumped in the passenger seat and greeted me with a big smile.

"I'm so glad you agreed to help us with this case," she said as she buckled her seat belt. "You are the most down to earth and accurate psychic medium we've worked with."

The trunk door slammed as Jason and the crew loaded the last of the equipment into the car.

"Jason will be taking a lot of back roads and a roundabout way to get to our location. This is to hopefully prevent you from knowing where we are going. We don't want you to get any preconceived notions or be accused of researching the area before we get there."

I had become accustomed to this drill.

I nodded in agreement and looked out the car window, imagining where this journey would lead. It was six o'clock, and the late

June sun was still shining, creating a cast of shadows over the undulating terrain. The investigation was to begin at eight o'clock and continue late, when the sun retired and the stillness of night would remove visual distractions, taking away light but enhancing the ability to hear, smell, and feel.

I had met the team of paranormal investigators only two months ago during a fundraising event for a local historical society. The team raised money by charging people a fee to participate in an investigation of a historical home that was said to be haunted. My husband and I paid the fee and attended the event. We were among the first group of the evening to conduct the investigation and arrived at our destination a few minutes prior to the 6 p.m. scheduled time. We parked our car on the quiet, tree-lined road in front of the historic home. A woman wearing jeans and a black T-shirt with the paranormal team logo on the upper left corner stood waiting on the sidewalk. Her short, dark curls glistened in the evening sun, and her teeth gleamed as she met us with a warm, welcoming smile.

"I'm Kerry, one of the investigators," she said. "Come inside the house. We're meeting in the living room and will be given a brief tour by someone from the Historical Society before we begin the investigation."

We followed Kerry through the white, arched doorway of the 1848 Federal brick house. The Historical Society displayed county artifacts, antiques, and memorabilia throughout the building. As I stood waiting in the front room, my eyes scanned rosewood tables with marble centers, a grandfather clock with its pendulum swinging, a large spinning wheel, Victorian red velvet sofas and a large, ornate Victorian mourning wreath made of human hair, hung prominently on the parlor wall.

I walked across the room to get a closer look at the wreath. It was enclosed in an oval shadow box protected by a piece of glass. The hair of the wreath was intricately woven into a horseshoe-shaped string of hair bouquets with a large mass of hair flowers placed in the middle. The blending of different hair shades made me wonder if this wreath had been made with the combination of hair from many deceased people. The top of the hair horseshoe was not connected and remained open to symbolize the ascent towards heaven. Usually, the hair in the center of the wreath belonged to the most recently deceased family member and remained there until another family member died. It would then be pushed aside to make room for the hair of the newly departed. I found the mourning rituals of the Victorian period eerily fascinating, yet oddly familiar and comforting.

My attention was taken away from the wreath when a woman from the Historical Society and the paranormal investigative team joined us. The small-framed, white-haired woman introduced herself as Ann. She took us on a tour of the house and explained that the rooms at the back of the house were the original part of the building, which was the first one-room schoolhouse in the area and was in operation until 1822. The schoolhouse had a single room on the second floor that served as living quarters for the teacher. After the school closed, the house became a single-family home, with the brick part of the house added in 1848.

The tour ended on the second floor in a room filled with various technical equipment. We sat on folding chairs and were introduced to the investigative team of Kerry, Jason, Lonnie, Corey, and Matt. Lonnie and Corey were the techies. Lonnie's eyes sparkled with excitement beneath his thick, horned-rimmed glasses while he explained the different uses of the equipment. He stroked his auburn beard and stressed that all equipment had to be in position, ready to record, before the start of an investigation. They used digital voice recorders to capture any noises or voices. A DVR system with infrared cameras recorded movement in complete darkness. Digital thermometers and EMF (electromagnetic field) detectors documented EMF levels and temperatures.

Corey sat behind a table filled with computers, TV screens, and monitors. His demeanor was professional as he explained that a spirit may cause the EMF to spike or cause dips in temperatures. Corey stood and held out an audio recorder for us to see. His thin, tall physique added to his authoritative manner. His short, brown hair was neatly groomed, and his voice trembled a bit as he explained how digital audio recorders were used to collect and analyze audio data. The digital recorders helped to capture EVPs, electronic voice phenomena, which many believe are voices of spirit. They also are used to confirm audio data collected by the video cameras. Corey's main job was to analyze, debunk, and authenticate the data collected during an investigation.

After the introduction to all the equipment, the lights in the house were turned off. Before we followed Kerry and Jason out of the equipment room, I opened my purse and took out the only equipment I planned on using — the dowsing rods I had purchased in Gettysburg.

Ever since my introduction to the dowsing rods, I found that they acted as an antenna to help me tune in the spirit world. I also found that energy could manipulate the rods to point to important areas within an investigation scene. I would let the rods lead the way. The rods moved quickly and deliberately, leading me to various rooms in the house and helping me connect to the imprinted energy left behind from the souls of long ago.

It was during our investigation of the kitchen that I immediately felt the presence of a woman. She was very proud of her home and was also very annoyed that my husband sat at her kitchen table before he was invited. She enjoyed her time cooking, baking for the neighborhood children, and keeping a nice home. She told me that her husband was also in the house and spent most of his time upstairs, especially when others were present. When speaking of her husband, she became nervous and clearly did not want to upset him. I felt his energy controlling her a bit. When I asked if we could take pictures, she became nervous and told me not to. Taking pictures would upset him. Her husband was extremely guarded and annoyed that we were in his home. His energy made it clear that he did not want any part of our investigation or to accommodate us with pictures. He was overwhelmed and anxious because of the crowd in his house. He was stoic, apprehensive, and nervous.

This man clearly believed "what goes on in this house, stays in this house."

The investigation lasted more than two hours. We had to leave promptly when our time was finished to allow the 9 p.m. group to begin their investigation. It had been a fun experience, and I was able to share some interesting findings with the team.

"Hello. This is Corey from the paranormal investigative team," the voice on the other end of the phone said. It had been two weeks since the fundraiser, and Corey's call was a surprise.

"Hi Corey!" I said. "I really enjoyed the investigation and was impressed by the professionalism of your team."

"Thank you. I'm calling because our team was impressed with you. I've completed analyzing the data we collected from your investigation. I would like to send you an EVP that was captured while you were communicating with spiritual energy in the kitchen. It's a class A recording and is very clear. The recording is evidence that you were communicating and also getting accurate information. In addition to the EVP, we have researched the family who owned the home. We also interviewed people who are related to the family and people who knew them. The man and woman you described fit the description of Mr. and Mrs. Smith, the original owners of the home. In fact, the way you described their personalities and their relationship was extremely accurate, according to family members and records."

Corey took a breath before he continued. "Our team has worked with psychics and mediums before, but there's something different about you. You are real. We're wondering if you would be interested in working with us and helping us out on some cases."

My jaw dropped. I had not expected this. "Of course, I would love to work with you!"

"Great!" Corey responded. "I'll email you the EVP so you can hear it for yourself. I'll also email upcoming investigation dates. These investigations are strictly confidential. There may be some investigations where we will be working with other teams or law enforcement. I'm only sending you the dates and times. You won't receive any other information except a location to meet us on the day of the investigation. We'll provide the transportation to the location."

"Yes, of course. That makes sense," I agreed as my head scrambled to wrap itself around our conversation.

"Thank you. We look forward to working with you," Corey said.

"Thank you, and I look forward to working with you, as well!"

After I hung up, my husband and I sat at the desk in our home office, waiting for the email. When it arrived we immediately played the EVP. In the recording I could be heard asking the spirit energy of the wife if we could take a picture of her and her husband. Right after my question we heard as clear as day the ghostly whisper of a disembodied voice stating "No! Don't!" The next voice heard was mine stating "No. Don't. They do not want their pictures taken. The husband would not like that." This was captured on video, as well. Evidence. Wasn't this one of the things I needed to validate my journey?

Jason opened the driver's side door and got behind the steering wheel. "Ready to go?" Kerry and I both answered yes as Jason backed the car from the driveway and steered us in the direction of our destination. The voice of spirit had once again led me to a new adventure.

Chapter 30: Grand Entrance to a New Place

Transform your thoughts and embrace love as a way of life. Your soul's dance is one of great joy and by acknowledging its beauty you foster the awakening spirit and create positive outcomes in all aspects of life. The essence of being alive is to live like you mean it and transform limiting beliefs. By doing so you inspire the heart which will in return guide you along a path of bliss to a happy and passionate life. — Spiritual Consultant Michael Teal

I opened the door to the large home and saw the group of people sitting at the dining room table. Dinner had already begun. I quickened my pace, not noticing the steps to the sunken living and dining room area. I made my grand entrance by gracefully stumbling in to meet my fellow writers.

All eyes were now upon me as I regained control of my balance and retrieved the sandal that had flown from my foot. I smiled and said, "Hi! I'm Diane."

The last to arrive.

I thought I would have plenty of time to drive from the Phoenix, Arizona, airport to the retreat house in Sedona. I had reserved my rental car to eliminate the hassle of doing it once I landed. I handed my reservation receipt to the overly smiling woman behind the rental counter in the crowded airport. She eagerly took my receipt and began punching information into her computer. I watched as her smile lessened the longer she stared at the screen. When she lifted her eyes to meet mine, her smile returned as she handed my reservation back to me.

"I am so sorry," she said in a voice that was all too sunny for someone who was supposedly feeling regret. Her bright pink lipstick had smeared across her teeth, and it was all I could do to stop myself from reaching over the counter with a tissue to wipe it away.

"We do not have a car reserved for you here at the airport. Your car is reserved at our sister site, which is approximately thirty miles from here."

Now I not only wanted to wipe the pink from her teeth, but the smile from her face.

"What sister site?" I asked in a tone that knocked her smile from a ten to a five. "Why would I reserve a car thirty miles from the airport?"

She increased her smile to an eight as she explained that there were no cars available at the airport similar to the one I reserved. I could conveniently take a taxi to their other location and pick up the car there.

"Do you have a shuttle to get me there?" I asked as I took a deep breath in an effort to remain calm.

"No. You would have to take a cab. It's the start of rush hour now so you will most likely hit some traffic, which means you'll probably reach our other rental site in an hour to an hour and a half."

"Is this rental site on the way to Sedona?" I asked hopefully.

No. The car rental site was in the opposite direction of Sedona. Expect an additional two hours to the already two-plus hour drive to Sedona. I didn't have that time to spare.

"That won't work. I need to be in Sedona by 6 p.m. What do you have at this site that I could rent?"

The rental agent tucked her bleached blond hair behind her ears and turned her smile back to a ten.

"We have a beautiful, top of the line luxury car that you can have at the price of eight hundred dollars, not including tax, miles and any additional fees."

I almost fell over. That was four times the price of my reserved car.

"What do you have comparable to my reserved car?" I said.

"Nothing. This is all we can offer you here. Perhaps if you call our 800 reservation service they can work something out for you."

The agent's smile was now gone, and she was eagerly looking at the customer in line behind me. According to her smile meter, my time was up. I knew it was time to move on, and I asked for a manager.

Clearly I must be aging when the people in positions of power begin to look like teenagers to me. If I had to guess, the car rental manager was sixteen. After explaining my situation, he very cheerfully apologized for the mix-up, and for my inconvenience he would deduct fifty dollars from the price of an eight-hundred-dollar rental. What card would I like to use?

Ugh! I graciously declined his bait and switch offer. I left the manager and stood in line at the competitor's kiosk. The lovely lady behind the counter listened patiently as I told her my tale of woe.

"This happens all the time," she said as she shook her head and started entering information in her computer. "These rental agencies get away with it because we're in the airport."

I watched her click away at the keyboard, biting her lip as she read the computer screen. "There is no way I can get you a deal even close to your initial reservation. I can give you a luxury car at our mid-sized price. It's four hundred dollars."

Although twice the price of my original reservation, it was half the price of the other quote. "I'll take it!"

I had looked forward to driving into Sedona while the sun was setting over the red rocks, causing the formations to glow in brilliant orange and red, a view I was told I should not miss. But my rental car fiasco had cost me more than an hour of valuable time, causing me to arrive in Sedona after the sun had set. And so I found myself stumbling into the writing retreat house hours later than planned.

After making my grand entrance, everyone laughed and informed me that I was just in time for introductions. Great. I wasn't sure how to introduce myself now without an academically approved titled. Diane. That was my title. Diane, the child who had recently been released from the protective barriers of my soul and the woman I was still discovering. I would own her. Being Diane was enough.

My eyes scanned the already crowded dining area, searching for a place to sit. Someone brought a chair from the kitchen and directed the group to make room for me at the table. As I approached my fellow writers, I was stopped by a woman who stood directly in front of me. She looked me in the eyes and said, "You are *that woman*!"

I recognized her right away from her picture on the website. It was Lisa, the writing coach of the retreat.

"I remember reading your work and loved it," Lisa said. "You are the one I'm really looking forward to meeting with!"

A well-known author, editor, and writing coach read and liked my writing. My fear now turned to unbridled excitement, and I was looking forward to getting feedback on my work.

I squeezed into a place at the table and listened to the introductions of this eclectic group of writers who came from Canada, California, Georgia, Pennsylvania, New Jersey, and other states to share their writing, hone their craft, network, and hopefully develop some lasting relationships, all while discovering more about themselves.

Writing a book had been something I had thought about doing as a young girl. After reading SE Hinton's books during my pre-adolescence, at the age of twelve I strived to write a story that rivaled The Outsiders. The thought of actually writing a novel didn't resurface until the summer of 2012 as I sat on the beach of the lake near my home, writing in my journal. There was something about the warm sunshine and being surrounded by nature that allowed the thoughts in my head to flow easily onto the paper. The journaling experience for me has been about releasing and working through unresolved issues, allowing me to better understand myself and move forward in my life. Journaling allows me to process and understand the circumstances of my life. By the time I complete a journal entry, I actually feel free. I had been journaling regularly now for two years. My journals had become my close friends with whom I shared and bared my soul. Journaling has been instrumental in my journey.

After sitting for hours on the beach that day, I put my pen down and stretched. A warm breeze blew though my hair, and I closed my eyes. Suddenly, Emelyn Hartridge came to my mind. I embraced her, now knowing her on a different level.

"Thank you for sharing your story with me," I said to her. "You were the catalyst that led me on my journey that changed the course of my life."

Emelyn put her finger to her lips, indicating the "be quiet" sign. I listened. "This is your story," she said. "It is yours to tell ... Please share it."

I opened my eyes and looked at the journal sitting on my lap. The old chatter entered my head: "Who would want to read this story?"

I quickly stopped the self-doubt and refused to listen to it any more. I now knew how to turn off the internal negative dialogue. I now knew how to listen to my inner voice, my gut, my higher self— to spirit. I now knew how to trust.

I opened my journal to a new page and began to write:

"It was an evening in July, the summer I slowed down enough to listen, when I was hit with a daunting question: When and how did I become *That Person*?"

That was the beginning of writing my story with the intention to share it with others.

A year later I found myself on the other side of the United States, sitting with published authors, editors, and fellow newbies, looking to create and manifest dreams of writing and publishing to reality.

I sat at the dining room table of the retreat house, eating and listening to the writers one-by-one share a brief glimpse of themselves and explain why they were at the retreat. A young woman wearing a black fedora with a small feather attached to the left side introduced herself. Her dark, straight hair peeked out from beneath her hat, just reaching her shoulders. Her black-rimmed glasses could not hide the depth of her brown eyes nor could her dark plaid shirt, zipped-up sweatshirt, and dark jeans hide the depth of her spirit. Looking at the sea of faces around the table, it was easy for me to see that this woman was the youngest of the group. My instinct told me that, despite her youth, she was an old soul. She introduced herself as Krista and shared that she had two dog children, one named Stevie, after her favorite musical artist, Stevie Nicks. That sealed the deal for me. Stevie Nicks had long been a favorite of mine, and I would play her music as inspiration while I wrote. In spite of our age difference, I knew we were meant to know one another.

Krista lived in Sedona and would leave the retreat house throughout the day to go home and tend to her dogs. She was quiet, and like me, would listen more than share. However, I knew that Krista had much to share even though she was only in her twenties. Her writing was deep and beautiful. Although she worked as an editor for a magazine, it was clear to me her true calling was to write. Only an old soul who had experienced life could write like Krista.

I began referring to Krista as my "hipster-sister," and by the end of the retreat we were calling each other soul sisters. The last night of the retreat, the group sat outside, circled around the fire pit that warmed us from the cool October air. It was here that we shared our experiences during the retreat. It was here that we wished each other well and said our goodbyes.

I had stepped outside my comfort zone by attending this retreat to explore my inner writer, to find the courage to share my work and yet again trust the guidance of spirit to lead me on another journey of self-discovery. It was during this last evening together that Krista and I promised to stay connected.

I had no idea how strong this connection would be or where it would lead.

Part III: Reiki

A healer's power stems not from any special ability, but from maintaining the courage and awareness to embody and express the universal healing power that every human being naturally possesses. — Eric Micha'el Leventhal

Chapter 31: Surprise Visit

Man learns through experience, and the spiritual path is full of different kinds of experiences. He will encounter many difficulties and obstacles, and they are the very experiences he needs to encourage and complete the cleansing process. — *Sai Baba*

"Krista is coming!" my husband announced as he sat at the desk and read through emails.

It was July. Nine months had passed since the writing retreat. I had stayed in touch with several of my fellow writers but had invited three women from the retreat to visit me in New Jersey. One was Krista. We had planned on going into New York City to see a Broadway show, spend time catching up, and support each other on our writing projects. Two of the women had committed to coming, but Krista had not been able to. Her mother was battling cancer. Krista was spending her time caring for her. She couldn't commit to coming to New Jersey.

"What?" I squealed in response to my husband's announcement.

How could this be? The women were arriving here in two days. According to her email, Krista would be here in three. It was a last-minute decision, but she was coming. She had bought the plane ticket. I was delighted.

It started soon after Krista arrived. The other two women from the retreat came with me to pick Krista up from the airport. We pulled up to the arriving flights of Southwest Airlines and found Krista waiting outside the terminal. We quickly put her luggage in the trunk, and she jumped in the back seat with Mary. I deliberately had the radio in the car turned off so the four of us could chat and catch up without distraction. It wasn't long after Krista entered the car and we approached the highway that the car radio came on without being touched. I was almost willing to brush it off, assuming I must have accidentally touched a button that controlled the radio. But even though the radio was tuned to a nearby station, nothing but loud static and white noise came booming from the speakers. I quickly apologized to the women and made sure the radio was completely turned off.

I didn't dismiss the incident but didn't mention it to the other women, either. I continued driving, laughing, and chatting, while putting the odd radio incident in the back of my mind. Before reaching home, it happened again. This time the radio was even louder. Once again, although tuned to a local radio station, music did not come blaring from the speakers. Instead, loud static and white noise disrupted our discussion.

"What's going on with your car radio?" Mary said.

"I'm not quite sure," I said. Yet deep inside I knew.

The next day we planned on visiting Two Buttons, the warehouse store owned by Elizabeth Gilbert, author of Eat, Pray, Love. Elizabeth and her husband had filled a warehouse in Frenchtown, New Jersey, with beautiful handmade objects from Java, Bali, India, and Thailand. The items in this warehouse were for sale to the public. Frenchtown is a wonderful little village on the Delaware River, right across the water from Bucks County, Pennsylvania, and about a forty-five minute drive from my home.

Once again we piled in the car, and I made sure the car radio was turned off. About halfway to our destination, blaring white noise and static came throbbing through the car speakers. I had not touched the radio. No one had turned it on, and once again the radio was tuned to a station that should have been playing music or at least a commercial. I turned down the volume and tuned the radio to another station just to make sure it was working. Music began to fill the silence in the car. The radio was working. I quickly turned off the radio and tuned in to my GPS that was giving me directions to our destination.

We spent hours browsing and shopping in the enormous warehouse of Two Buttons. Being there was like traveling the world in a single afternoon. After Two Buttons, we crossed over to New Hope, Pennsylvania, where we enjoyed a delicious lunch and more sightseeing. As we traveled back to my house, I double-checked to make sure that the radio was turned off. At some point during our trip home, the static white noise came blaring through the car speakers. The radio had once again turned on by itself and was not playing music.

"I can't ignore this any longer," I said. "Ever since we picked you up from the airport, Krista, the radio has turned on by itself and played loud static. I know there's someone from the other side trying to speak with you."

I looked in my rearview mirror and watched as Krista's face became perplexed. "That's interesting," she said. "I don't doubt you, but I really don't have anyone that was close to me who died. I can't imagine who it could be."

I dropped the subject, but I knew this was a message for Krista. I knew that if I listened, the message would come through.

The following day we all went to the lake by my house. We packed sandwiches, drinks, and our writing materials so we could spend the day on the beach eating, writing, and sharing. While sitting on the beach, I felt a strong presence around Krista. I put my pen down and took a deep breath. We had been working hard on our writing projects and brainstorming career opportunities, but I needed to address the activity surrounding Krista. I allowed myself to tap into the spirit world and discovered that the strong energy around Krista was a male. He was her grandfather. He was not from the United States and spoke German. Thankfully the language of spirit is universal, coming in thoughts, feelings, pictures, sounds, visions, and smells, making it possible for me to understand messages in any language. Her grandfather appeared as a handsome man with darker hair, wearing a military uniform. He came across as strict, stoic, and in urgent need to get a message through to Krista.

"Krista, can I share something about the spirit who is with you now?" I asked. I knew Krista was spiritual and open to this world, but I always ask first.

"Sure," she said. "Go for it, but I can't imagine who it would be. As I said, I really don't have anyone close to me who has passed away."

"Well, there is a very strong grandfather energy with you. He speaks German and didn't live in the United States. He's wearing a military uniform and is coming across as a stern and strict man. He's anxious and needs his message to be heard."

"My grandfather?" Krista said, obviously puzzled. "My mother's father was German and lived in Germany. He also was in the military, but why would he come to me? I never knew him."

I knew that sitting on a public beach was not the place to continue this conversation and suggested that after dinner at my home we could explore it further. With that, we packed up our belongings and headed back to my house.

Chapter 32: A Grandfather Reaches Out

The Soul holds the secret to healing. To listen, quiet the mind. — Anonymous

I lit the candles, burned sage, and turned on the calming music. Dinner was complete, and Krista was patiently waiting for me to set up my office in preparation for her Reiki session. Reiki is a healing technique that channels energy by means of touch and helps restore a person's physical and emotional wellbeing. Caring and worrying about her mother's health had left Krista emotionally and physically drained. Often when I perform a Reiki treatment I receive messages from the world of spirit. I had decided to do Reiki on Krista to help her heal as well as receive messages from her grandfather.

Krista entered my dimly lit office and sat on the twin bed that I was using as a Reiki table. I instructed her to lie on her back and take three deep breaths. Starting at the crown of Krista's head, I gently placed my hands on her skull. With my eyes closed, I connected with my source of energy and asked for guidance with this healing session. Soon a vision of bright light appeared in my mind from which an image of a man emerged. His rigid stance complemented his military attire, which accented his tall, slender build. Underneath the brim of his military cap I could see his strong, handsome face, his sharp, piercing eyes, and I could feel his sense of urgency. I knew this was Krista's grandfather. He began to pace.

I moved my hands to the next Reiki position, and Krista's grandfather stood still. He then reached out, took the hand of a woman, and brought her forward. The two of them stood together like statues.

"I see them!" Krista exclaimed as she continued lying on her back with her eyes closed. "I saw my grandfather reach out and bring my grandmother to him. I knew my grandmother. They are standing together. I now know for sure it is my grandfather. It's my mother's father."

I, too, was excited. It is such validation when someone else can see or feel the spiritual experience.

"Amazing!" I responded. "What you're seeing is also what I saw. Continue to relax, and I'll continue the Reiki treatment. Let's see what messages he has to share."

Although stern, his pinched lips and furrowed brow indicated concern. In the physical world, he was not a man to show affection. He was not a man to apologize. Yet it was coming through clearly to me that he had many apologies and regrets he wanted to share with his daughter, Maria. I took a deep breath and allowed myself to feel his turmoil. He regretted the strained relationship he had with his daughter. He regretted that even at the time of his death their relationship was distraught, leaving no time for reconciliation. He wanted Maria to know that he forgave her for leaving Germany. That he understood her. That he loved her. That he was sorry.

The grandfather then showed himself in a large white apron. He held up his hands, revealing that they were covered in dough. He apologized for making Maria work so hard as a young girl. He apologized for the ways he disciplined her. He now wanted to be part of Maria's healing. He wanted to connect to his daughter and mend the wounds between them. He wanted her to find peace. He wanted her to know how he felt. He wanted me to be the bridge that connected him to his daughter. He wanted me to go to Maria's home in Phoenix and give her five days of Reiki treatment.

When the Reiki session was finished, Krista and I sat in the stillness of my office, and I shared with her the messages I received.

She said her grandfather's apron and dough made sense. He had owned one of the finest bakeries in his town. Maria had worked endless hours there while going to school and helping her mother care for the house and her siblings.

Krista explained how her mother and grandfather did not get along. Maria dreamed of moving to America. Her dream came true when she married a U.S. soldier stationed in Germany and moved to California with him. Krista acknowledged that the relationship her mother had with her grandfather left a hole in her mother's heart.

"Your grandfather wants me to go to Phoenix and give your mother five days of Reiki treatments. He wants to connect with her. Would your mother be open to this?" I asked with hesitation.

Without hesitation, Krista replied, "Yes!"

Before I could respond, Krista was down the stairs, phone in hand, speaking with her mother.

"For the first time I can remember, my mother let down her wall and cried. She was overwhelmed with happiness to hear from her father and told me that she recently had been thinking about him. She has been praying to her mother for help. The cancer and her unresolved issues with her father have been a burden on her heart and on her soul. She's extremely excited and open to this experience. Will you really come to Phoenix?"

This time I did not hesitate. "Of course I will. I would be honored."

Chapter 33: Return to Sedona

If we accept our task to be the enlightened beings of our planet, we can begin to change the world. — Dr. Brian Weiss

The hot mid-September air nearly took my breath away as I exited the Phoenix airport. A tall, slender woman standing near a car at the designated pickup area was waving her hand to me. It didn't take me long to realize it was Maria. Her tall, lean physique resembled that of her father's. I quickly rolled my suitcase in her direction, placed my bag in the open trunk and slid into the passenger seat of the car. This was our first meeting, yet the moment I looked in her eyes, I felt as though we had known each other for years. Maria thanked me for coming, and her strong German accent took me by surprise.

Before long, we were on the highway headed to Sedona. Maria wanted her Reiki experience to be as spiritual and as healing as possible, so what better place than Sedona, which is considered one of the most healing and spiritual places in the United States. Maria had rented a three bedroom vacation home for us. Krista would meet us at the house this evening.

We chatted for the entire two-hour car ride, covering a vast array of subjects such as music, parenting, and travel. Maria was a strong soul who had been battling breast cancer for two years. She wore an ash-blond wig to hide her hair loss from her treatments and a beautiful, warm smile to hide her pain. Maria shared that her marriage to Krista's father did not last, and she soon found herself as a single parent, in a foreign country, working hard to support her family. The connection I made with Maria took away the nervous anxiety I had been feeling about this trip.

The Arizona sun was setting just as we approached the Sedona red rocks. This time I would not miss it. The illumination of the setting sun gave the rocks a spectacular glow, creating the most colorful works of art made by nature. I watched as the blues, reds, oranges, and pinks painted pictures across the sky and faded away as the sun sank behind the mountains. It was beautiful. It was surreal. It was spiritual.

Maria pulled the car into the driveway. The adobe-style ranch house was nestled in the foothills of the red rocks, providing wondrous views in all directions. Krista heard the car door slam shut and came outside to greet us. We unloaded the car and brought our things into the house.

The family room was the main focal point, with its large stone fireplace providing warmth during the cool Sedona evenings. The modern kitchen and dining room overlooked the sunken family room, giving an open, spacious feeling to the home. The sliding glass doors to the rear of the family room opened to an outdoor eating area and hot tub. The bedrooms flanked both sides of the family room, each with its own private bath. It was the perfect location for our healing adventure.

Since it was getting late and we were tired from our day of travel, we agreed to go out for dinner and begin our Reiki sessions in the morning, when we were refreshed. That night, I sunk into bed, exhausted yet looking forward to discovering what would take place the next day. As I put my head on the pillow, thoughts started racing through my head: What if her father doesn't come through? What if I traveled all this way only to disappoint Maria and let down Krista? After all that I've experienced, was I still in doubt? Just the same, what if her father does come through? What if their relationship heals? It was out of my hands. Out of my control. Yet I knew the truth. I drifted off to sleep knowing that spirit doesn't lie. I trusted that the energy of spirit would provide what was needed. It had so far.

Chapter 34: A Family Affair

A healer's power stems not from any special ability, but from maintaining the courage and awareness to embody and express the universal healing power that every human being naturally possesses. — Eric Micha'el Leventhal

I opened the bedroom door to find Krista pacing right outside of it.

"You have been in there for nearly three hours!" Krista announced with a concerned tone to her voice. "You said a Reiki treatment is sixty to ninety minutes! I was getting ready to open the door and check on the two of you. Is everything okay?"

Everything was fine. But how was I to explain this experience? An experience that felt as though it occurred within a blink of an eye, but in reality went on for nearly three hours? An experience that defied time and brought us both to another realm. An experience that could not be justly described in mere words.

There was no doubt that Maria's father was orchestrating our Reiki sessions. From the moment I awoke, he had been dictating instructions to me. Before I could begin Reiki on Maria, her father informed me that I needed to incorporate specific items into each session to enhance the experience. In addition to burning sage, he wanted sweet grass burned and rose quartz crystals placed around Maria during the Reiki sessions. I had never used these items and didn't have them, but I knew I needed to find them. Maria's father made it clear that there was no compromising, and if I was going to do the job, I needed to do it the right way, meaning his way.

I told Krista about the directions from her grandfather. She laughed. It was no surprise to her. Her grandfather was a controlling man who lived by the motto: "If you are going to do something, do it right the first time." After breakfast, Krista brought me into the town of Sedona to purchase the necessary materials.

I wandered through the spiritual gift shop with amazement. The store was a metaphysical resource for healers. I didn't know where to begin. There was a large section of the store dedicate to crystals, so I decided to start there. As I approached the area, I noticed a chart displayed near the vast array of stones that gave a description of each crystal and its use. After reading the chart, it was no surprise that Maria's father wanted to surround his daughter with rose quartz. This specific crystal is said to align with the heart chakra, governing emotions, especially love. It can be used to nurture, attract love, and promote self-acceptance. It is also known to be extremely supportive for mending a broken heart as well as strengthening the bond between child and parent.

After carefully choosing several rose quartz crystals, I wandered over to the sage products. The store carried just about any type or mix of sage one could imagine. But I was looking for sweet grass, and since I had never seen it before, I didn't exactly know what to look for.

Krista joined me by the sage display.

"I'm looking for sweet grass," I said.

Krista and I both scanned the shelves, but found no sweet grass.

Krista's left leg began to shake. "I don't know why," she said, "but there's a strange tingling sensation running through my leg."

She bent over to massage the strange feeling out of her leg and came to a sudden stop. There in a basket next to her leg were long braids of sweet grass. As soon as she noticed the sweet grass, the sensation in her leg disappeared.

I purchased the items, and we headed back to the house, where I would perform the first of five Reiki treatments.

The treatments took place in my bedroom of the rented house. I lit the candles, burned the sweet grass, and played calming music designed for Reiki practice. As Maria lay on the bed, I applied the appropriate Reiki symbols, called for guidance from spirit, and instructed Maria to take three deep "yoga" breaths.

The aroma of the sweet grass soon filled the room with a scent that reminded me of the smell of a prairie after a fresh spring rain.

A smile came across Maria's face.

"I know why my Dad wanted you to burn the sweet grass," she said. "It smells just like the meadows in Germany. It reminds me of my childhood."

With closed eyes, I placed my hands on the crown of Maria's head. Almost instantly, a strong, cold breeze entered the room, and the shiver of Maria's body was validation that I was not the only one to experience the change in temperature. One by one I could feel Maria's loved ones enter the room from the world of spirit. My mind showed me a male at Maria's feet who introduced himself as her uncle. At her left shoulder, a sweet and loving woman came through as her aunt. At Maria's right shoulder stood her mother. A younger woman carrying a serving tray of food and drink appeared circling around Maria and claimed to be a dear friend. Last, but not least, Maria's father appeared above her, clearly in a position of authority.

From that point on, I experienced an outer body whirlwind that took me on a healing journey of love. There was no doubt that I was a vessel being used to allow Maria's loved ones to come forward and bridge the gap that was not filled while they were here in the physical world. That aching gap had caused Maria pain throughout the years. Her loved ones were determined to heal it so Maria could move forward.

The best part of the treatments was what Maria experienced. She, too, felt the cool breeze as her relatives and friend from spirit entered the room. She, too, saw them take position around her each time I placed my hands on her head to begin the session. Maria felt as if she had been wrapped in a healing cocoon of love.

Many messages were shared, released, and recovered. The uncle who took his place at Maria's feet reminded her of a letter he had written that she had taken out of a trunk in her parents' attic during her last visit to Germany. He wanted her to find the letter and read the last paragraph. Maria had admired her uncle. He was the first to leave Germany and begin a new life in the United States. She had planned to join him once she was old enough. Unfortunately, her uncle's life was cut short before this could happen. Maria had forgotten about the letter, but the memory came flooding back. When Maria returned to her home in Phoenix, she immediately found the letter. The last paragraph contained encouraging words of love and support for her. It was a gentle reminder that she was loved, a reminder Maria greatly needed considering that she had lived for many years feeling otherwise.

The aunt who kept her position at Maria's left shoulder was a loving soul who offered nurturing and comforting support. She brought forward fond memories of Maria running through the grassy fields near her home in Germany and resting beneath the cool shade of an apple tree. She reminded Maria of the tulips and daffodils they planted together and how they each would become breathless at the sight of the boldly colored blooms. Her aunt inspired Maria to reconnect with her creative side, encouraging her to continue with her knitting, her scrap-booking, her card making, and any other project that brought her peace and joy.

The friend that appeared each session would spend her energy bopping around Maria to make sure all was well, lending support and levity where needed. Maria explained that this was her good friend from Germany, Bobbi, who passed away too soon from breast cancer. It was no surprise that she came through, constantly on the move, with a tray of food and drink in hand. This was the way she was in life, a great hostess who enjoyed entertaining guests, ensuring everyone's glasses were filled with alcohol, their stomachs were filled with food, and their hearts were filled with love.

Maria's mother never left her side. She appeared at her right shoulder, and that is where she stayed, holding Maria's hand, rubbing her arm, wiping her brow, and humming songs from Maria's childhood. She was a sustaining force, providing unconditional love and support for her daughter, a love that Maria felt throughout the Reiki sessions.

Maria's father acted as Commander in Chief throughout each session. Each day of Reiki seemed to have a specific theme: Love, forgiveness, self-care, physical healing, and new beginnings. Her father would telepathically communicate the goal of each session, and messages came through that aligned with the daily goal. Within these five days, Maria's father was able to convey his love for his daughter. He made amends for being a staunch disciplinarian and not being more accepting of Maria's dreams and choices. He guided Maria on a recall of pleasant memories from her childhood, reinforcing the good and diminishing the negative feelings that were harbored in her soul. He loved her. He accepted her. He healed the wounds between them. I did not need to tell Maria this. She herself felt and experienced it during each Reiki session.

During one session, her father gave me instructions to repeat a phrase to Maria. I couldn't understand the phrase because it was in German, but I did understand the love and importance of the words. After the Reiki ended, I did my best to repeat the words that were so important for her father to share.

"Maria, I don't know if this will even make sense to you, but your father wants me to tell you something, and it's very important to him that I say it in German," I said, hoping I could pull this off. "I'll do my best to repeat what I heard, and I hope you'll understand what I'm attempting to say. He said 'eek lea ba deek.'"

I knew my pronunciation was off, but I hoped it was close enough to translate.

Maria started crying, and Krista just sat on the family room couch, staring at me.

"I do know what he is saying, and I know why he wanted you to say it in German. It's something I've always wanted to hear from my father, yet these are words he did not speak. It's pronounced 'ich liebe dich,' and it is German for 'I love you.' I can't begin to explain how much this means to me. It's all I ever wanted him to say."

The wounds of her inner child had been acknowledged. True healing was underway.

Chapter 35: A Turn for the Worse

It is through gratitude for the present moment that the spiritual dimension of life opens up. —Eckhart Tolle

M*arch 9 at 1:22 pm. The private message sent via Facebook read: I have been very sick with dehydration and malnutrition. What does my pops say about this? Tell him I'm scared.*

My heart sank. It had been sixth months since I first met Maria for our retreat in Sedona. We had kept in contact, and things had been going well. I read the message again. I couldn't wrap my head around it. I convinced myself she was all right. I convinced myself this was a passing episode, a brief setback. She had come too far for this to be anything major.

The Reiki experience provided Maria the time needed to quiet her mind and embrace the messages brought to her. It provided essential elements to allow love to grow, inviting new experiences to come forward. Maria had started a new life since our days together in Sedona. She was planning on selling her house in Phoenix and purchasing a home in Sedona. She was going to live closer to Krista and spend more time doing the things she loved. She was knitting again, crafting, and taking daily long walks. She stopped making "to-do" lists and instead was making herself a priority. She made peace with her father, which in turn created peace within her heart. How could things have changed so quickly?

In November, two months after we first met, Maria had surgery. The doctor removed 99 percent of the disease. I found this to be great news. I found this to be a sign that Maria had a long life to live. The day she came home from the hospital was the day I flew out to Phoenix to see her. What I saw when I entered the house was not what I had anticipated. There was Maria, sitting on the couch, smiling with her face aglow. Her once balding scalp now proudly displayed beautiful salt and pepper curls. The brightly colored tulips I had sent were placed in a vase on the table next to her, along with assorted novels and her latest knitting project. She radiated life and love.

During my stay in November, I gave Maria Reiki treatments. These treatments were very different from the treatments of three months ago. Wounds of the heart no longer needed mending, and the energy was very soothing. Maria's departed family was with me throughout the sessions, sending her healing love. The feeling of love was so strong that at times it overflowed and leaked out Maria's eyes in the form of tears.

The last evening of my stay, we went out to dinner. When I first arrived, I hadn't expected Maria to get out of bed, but here she was, looking beautiful, feeling strong, and walking into the restaurant with an air of confidence. She was ready to begin her new chapter of life.

Now, four months later, she was not well. She was scared.

I had just seen Krista in December, when she came to stay with us during the Christmas holiday. She hated to leave her mother, but her mother encouraged Krista to come spend time with us. Krista said her mom was doing well. She felt great. She looked great. She was taking long walks each day. She was knitting socks. She was the happiest she had been in a very long time. Life was good.

Krista, and I had made plans to fly to Louisiana in January and visit a fellow alum from the writing retreat. Unfortunately when January arrived, Krista hesitantly backed out, saying she could no longer commit to going away. Her initial reasons were that she had too many commitments and not enough money. But eventually she said, "My mother is starting chemo and radiation that week. I don't want to leave her."

I didn't think much of it at first. I thought it was routine. I thought it was a preventative measure. I thought she would be fine. Krista knew otherwise. Krista had disagreed with her mother's decision, and they had argued. Although she did not share it with me at the time, Krista knew that this treatment would be the beginning of the end.

Maria's slender body had not fully recovered from surgery when she began radiation and chemotherapy, at the advice of doctors, to eradicate the one percent of tissue that surgery had left behind. Krista stayed by her mother's side and supported her decision, although she did not agree, and watched as her mother's life deteriorated with each treatment she received.

Since the time I last saw Maria in November, I had believed she was well. I had believed she was growing stronger each day. It wasn't until I received her message on March 9 that I thought otherwise.

"My mother is going to die," Krista's voice on the other end of the phone informed me. "She's losing bladder control, which is a sign the end is near. I've been preparing myself for this over the last two months, which is why I've been withdrawn and not in contact lately. My mother doesn't want to see many people, but she keeps asking for you."

"I'll be there," I said as I grabbed my laptop and began looking up flights to Phoenix. "The best deal I can get is the end of next week. Will that work for you? If so, I'll book it."

Krista thought for a moment and said, "She's getting weaker each day and deteriorating quickly. She had a bad fall in the bathroom Friday night and hit her head. We've been in the hospital all weekend. The doctors ran tests. The cancer has spread to her liver and brain. I hope she'll still be coherent by the time you get here. She should be. Go ahead and buy the ticket."

As soon as we hung up from our conversation I filled out all the needed information to book my flight. Just as I was about to hit the final payment button, the phone rang. It was Krista again.

"Did you purchase your ticket yet?" she said.

"I was just about to hit the payment button when you called. Why?"

"I think that if we wait a week you'll be here just in time to help me plan the funeral. My mother wants and needs you here now. She's purchasing your ticket. The cost doesn't matter. Just get here."

Chapter 36: Full Circle

Spiritual relationship is far more precious than physical. Physical relationship divorced from spiritual is body without soul. —Mahatma Gandhi

"Brost!" shouted Oskar as we clinked the bottom of our glasses in a toast to honor Maria. I'm not a beer drinker, but for some reason the beer tasted better in Germany. I sat across from Maria's brother, Oskar, and watched in amazement as he skillfully poured a beer without allowing any foam to enter the glass. He had it down to an art, from the way he rolled the bottle prior to opening, to the way he poured the beverage in one clean swoop. Both German and English languages were being exchanged at the large wooden table in the outside courtyard of Maria's childhood home. It amazed me how the language barrier didn't stop us from communicating. Everyone at the table was fluent in the universal language of love, a love we shared for Maria.

Krista's intuition had been correct. If I had postponed my trip to Phoenix, I would have been too late.

Maria had just been released from the hospital when I arrived. The cool, gray, late March weather of New Jersey was far behind me as I breathed in the arid air of Arizona. From the flat desert rose the jagged rock formations of the Superstition Mountains. The glistening sun was trapped behind their craggy peaks as they challenged the sky, determined to reach heaven. The landscape surrounding Maria's home was dominated by these majestic mountains, giving a feeling of ominous protection. While I stood on her front porch, hesitant to open the door, a warm breeze grazed my neck as if the breath of the mountain range was injecting me with its strength.

I found Maria sitting in her living room surrounded by friends and loved ones. The beautiful curls covering her head had grown since I saw her last, and her skin still radiated the warm glow I had seen in November. I was relieved to see her so vibrant and did my best to convince myself that somehow this was a mistake. Somehow, Maria was going to get well. Somehow, Maria would be able to live the life she had planned.

I immediately joined Maria on the sofa and snuggled up against her. Occasionally, she would drift off to sleep, but not for long. She didn't want to miss what was going on around her. I didn't want to miss the opportunity to be around her.

How could I love someone so deeply that I had known for such a short period of time? There was a connection between us that could not be defined, an intimate connection fused by spirit and created in a realm where time cannot be measured. Through our Reiki sessions we shared an intimate experience that was ours. I saw her soul, and she saw mine. Although brief, our connection was timeless.

One by one the afternoon visitors said their goodbyes to Maria, leaving us with the haunting quiet of words not yet spoken. Maria held strong throughout the day, but the lids of her eyes were now heavy, and her body craved rest. She had been sitting on the couch all day, and it was time for her to retreat to the hospital bed that had recently been added to her bedroom. I lit candles, sage, and sweetgrass. I played her favorite music. I placed my hands on the crown of Maria's head and began Reiki. It wasn't long before I heard the sounds of gentle snoring, and knew she had drifted to sleep. Her family in spirit was once again with me during the Reiki session. However, this time was different. This time they were preparing Maria for entrance to a new world.

Her father was having difficulty with this task. He had wanted a different outcome. As in life, he still wanted to be in control of his daughter's destiny. Radiation and chemotherapy had not been part of his recent plan, just as watching his daughter move to the United States many years ago was not part of his plan. Yet he had to accept the gift of free will that was bestowed upon the human race, specifically his daughter. He had spent too many of his physical years trying to control Maria's free will with no success. He was not about to allow her free will to stand between their newly healed relationship. He needed to accept. He needed to receive his daughter with all his love and help make this experience as painless as possible.

"Please tell my dad I am sorry," Maria pleaded while I sat at her feet the next day, watching the liquid drip from the IV to her vein. She sat upright in the reclining chair, and her moist eyes met mine. I hadn't said a word about the way her father came across during last night's Reiki session. But she knew.

"I don't want him to be disappointed or upset with my decisions. I want him to love me."

I placed my head on her lap. "Nothing you can do will stop him from loving you. He knows that the decisions about your health are yours to make. He's proud of you. You have nothing to be sorry for."

Maria let out a deep sigh of relief, closed her eyes and allowed the waves of sleep to engulf her.

During Reiki that evening, I once again listened to the rhythmic breath of Maria's gentle snore. With closed eyes, I could see Maria's loved ones gather around her, and I could feel the strong need from her father to relay a message. I focused my energy on listening to him. I clearly heard the long, deep sound of bells as her father took my hand and led me down a cobblestone road in the direction of the melodious sound. Quaint bakeries, small markets, and private homes boasting magnificent flowers lined either side of this quiet road. Our pace slowed, and we stopped when we reached the church in the center of town. The vertical lines of the building directed my eyes towards the heavens where the graceful steeple was home to the large brass bell, responsible for the loud, clear ringing that echoed through the village. Adjoining the sanctuary was a modest churchyard. Maria's father once again took my hand and guided me through the rows of small grave plots, covered with beautiful flowers and plants. At the head of each plot was a stone, engraved with names of loved ones who were no longer here in the physical world. We stopped in front of a square plot that contained a large stone, gray in color with two columns on either side. Between the two columns was a plaque with the names of Maria's parents engraved at the top and her uncle and aunt at the bottom. A blank space in between was where Maria's father wanted his daughter's name to be added. This was the family plot. This is where Maria's father wanted her to be reunited with loved ones. He wanted his daughter to return to Germany.

"Tell Maria to listen for the church bells this coming Sunday. When she hears them, she knows it will be time to come home," her father said. "We will be waiting for her."

The morning sun was already in full strength as we packed the car to spend the day at the lake. Maria had wanted to see the water while she was still able. I wheeled the chair as close to the car as possible and watched as her significant other, Randy, lovingly helped Maria maneuver her frail body into the front passenger seat. In the forty-eight hours since my arrival, Maria's body had declined quickly, and the pillows that were carefully tucked around her frame offered little to eliminate her pain as we took the forty-five minute drive to be in the healing presence of water.

Randy was a great tour guide, educating us about the different flowering plants that adorned the desert landscape as we gazed out the car windows. While I sat in the back seat with Krista, I was suddenly hit with the realization that I had not mentioned anything about the family plot in Germany. I had not shared Maria's father's wishes.

Maria's body, propped with pillows, tilted toward the left as she dozed off to sleep. "Krista, do you know anything about a family plot in Germany?" I said, breaking the still silence that had crept over the car.

Krista's face twisted as she thought about my question. "No. I don't know anything about it, and it's not something my mom has mentioned. Randy, do you know anything about a family plot in Germany?"

Randy hesitated. "I really am not sure. There may be one. Why are you asking?'

I squirmed as doubt entered my thoughts. No one seemed to know about the plot, so what if it was just my imagination? Surely, it would have been something Maria would have mentioned. I pushed the doubt away, took a deep breath and told Krista and Randy about last night's Reiki experience. I described the church, the bells, the town, the grave, the stone, and the plaque. I shared her father's wishes.

"Amazing!" Krista announced. "I can't believe you waited this long to tell us!"

Maria was stirring from her sleep.

"Mom, do you know anything about a family burial plot in Germany?"

The initial haze from sedated sleep lifted from Maria's eyes as she quickly answered, "Yes. There is a plot. Both my parents are there."

Our eyes widened at this knowledge.

"Maria." Randy began in a tone that indicated what he was about to say was important. "Your father shared this information with Diane. He wants your ashes to be brought back to Germany and placed in the plot with your family. Is this something you would like?"

Without hesitation, Maria answered with a decisive "yes." "That is where I would like to be. I would like to be back with my parents."

"Do you know anything about a stone with your parents name's engraved on it?" Krista asked.

"Yes. I think there is a stone like that," Maria said.

"Your father would like your name on the stone with theirs. Do you want that?" Krista said.

"Absolutely!" Maria replied as if she was surprised and honored by her father's request.

"Then you have my word that we will make this happen," said Randy. And he did.

That evening, Randy did some research and found a picture of the family plot in Germany. It was just as I described. He contacted Maria's siblings in Germany and made all the arrangements. After that day, Maria's health deteriorated quickly.

I left Phoenix that Friday, only three days after our trip to the lake. I knew it would be the last time I saw Maria in the physical world. I wanted to stay through the weekend. I wanted to be with her as she took her last breath. Maria's last words to me were asking me not to go. I was torn, yet I knew it was time. I had promised my daughter I would be home for her dance competition. I had others depending on me.

"Listen for the church bells," I whispered in her ear. "When you hear them, it will be time to go home. Your parents will be waiting for you."

The silent tears of grief accompanied me throughout my flight back to New Jersey.

Sunday afternoon, while watching my daughter dance on stage, I received the text from Krista. Maria had passed. It happened just as her father had told me.

Three months after her death I found myself in Maria's hometown of Germany, surrounded by her family, celebrating her life. Randy generously included me in the trip that brought Maria full circle. A trip that brought her back to a country she had so desperately wanted to leave and back to a father she so desperately wanted to love.

The quiet German village was almost a replica of the one I had seen with Maria's father during our last Reiki session. The church with the bell tucked away in the large steeple was only a block from the family home, and it was the sound of this bell echoing through the town that called us to her graveside on the day of her service. Maria's name engraved on the stone just underneath her parents' names would serve as a tangible marker of the reunification of family. At last, his daughter had returned home. At last, she felt loved and accepted enough by her father to return home. Healing comes in many forms.

Epilogue

Sometimes letting things go is an act of far greater power than defending or hanging on. — *Eckhart Tolle*

As I stand in front of the group of adults who have gathered to take my class, I smile to think that my journey has brought me back to teaching. But does one ever really stop teaching? Aren't we all teachers? The energy of everything we do, everything we say, everything we touch, spreads into the universe and has an effect. Whether that effect is positive or negative strongly depends on our intentions.

My spiritual journey was a leap of faith that moved me forward from an ego-driven life to a life of reconnection to the soul and the acceptance of spirit. It has brought me to teaching others how to remove the barriers and walls that keep one in the pain of the past, preventing one from moving forward and embracing new opportunities. It was a journey that convinced me, without a doubt, that we are all connected and one with the universe. It is a non-ending, circular journey of remembering and returning to who and what I am. I am no longer walking through life, in a state of fear, not accepting that who I am is enough, but instead have shifted to a state of love and acceptance.

Finding Emelyn allowed me to let go of the past — the past from more than one hundred years ago and the past from this life. I believe that Emelyn's life was deeply embedded in my soul, pushing me to continue following a map set to a course I had already traveled. Emelyn came to me so strongly and brought me on her life journey so I could find the validation needed to give myself permission to let go, move forward and allow my soul to grow.

Reliving the past and holding on to its hurts, whether from this life or a previous one, can have detrimental effects to the human soul. The weight of the past can act as an anchor, tying us down, preventing us from living in the moment. Preventing us from being who we really want to be.

Eckhart Tolle said that people create and maintain problems because it gives them a sense of identity. Was I maintaining and recreating Emelyn's life as my own for fear of losing this identity? Was I afraid that I would not know who I would be if I followed a different path? Letting go is not easy. It requires leaving your comfort zone and coming face to face with your fears, pushing you to overcome the challenges as they present themselves, allowing you to once again take charge of your life. Finding Emelyn allowed me to do this. Finding Emelyn allowed me to find myself.

Experiencing abuse or neglect as a child can leave us feeling wounded, deprived, and wronged by those who were loved and trusted. Confronting my childhood memories was painful, but necessary to gain mastery over my past. The quiet, undisturbed moments of journal writing allowed me to objectively revisit what happened and see it from an adult perspective. I was able to get a better understanding of my parents' own struggles and access the past with love and understanding as opposed to hurt and fear. This understanding allowed me to move past the blame and tear down the walls I had built around my soul for protection. It allowed me to let go of the unhealthy relationships I had built with both my parents and instead develop new relationships with them, based on love, understanding and forgiveness.

I was also able to let go of the need to impress people with my various educational degrees, career status, and material belongings to win their acceptance and love. I was able to focus on accepting and loving myself. Letting go of the fear of rejection allowed me to dive into my mediumship. I could not do the work if the fear of what people thought of me took over. Fear and anxiety are roadblocks to the spirit world. My new career has provided me with the opportunity to meet so many wonderful and caring people and travel to many places I might not have seen. Instead of losing friends over my choices, I have gained so many more. Instead of feeling embarrassed and ashamed, I feel valued and respected. Instead of feeling judged and unloved, I feel accepted and connected.

Emelyn came at a time I most needed her. I knew running the school was too much for me. I knew the government was changing regulations and its position on my type of school. I also knew my ego would not let me back down and let go. I knew I was drowning and afraid to ask for help. Emelyn guided me, convincing me that it was not only okay to let go of the school, but that it was time. I had another purpose waiting for me.

My journey certainly has not ended, and I believe it never will. The spiritual journey is one of self-discovery, where the tough, uncomfortable questions we have avoided come to the surface and are the catalyst of our quest. There are no time restraints, due dates, or judgments.

Was I really Emelyn Hartiridge in another life? I will let you decide. Although no longer feeling strongly pushed to run an academic school for children, Emelyn is still a part of my life, gently reminding me of past accomplishments while encouraging me to live for the greater good. Finding Emelyn may have saved my life.

It is never too late to begin.

Alfred Lamar Hartridge

Emelyn Battersby Hartridge

Alfred's memorial

Emelyn's grave marker

Noble-Hardee Mansion – "The House"

Staircase inside "The House"

One of the Victorian homes in Savannah that Emelyn used for her school

A Victorian home I wanted to use for my school.

Apparition of a soldier in Gettysburg

The Pugs

My amazing daughter.

My Father and Aunt

Me, as a child, telling fortunes to raise money for the First Aid Squad.

My last picture with Maria.

Maria's grave in Germany.

www.ingramcontent.com/pod-product-compliance
Lightning Source LLC
Chambersburg PA
CBHW031129090426
42738CB00008B/1022

* 9 7 8 1 9 4 9 0 0 1 2 2 8 *